The
Horse Keeper's
Handbook

THE
HORSE KEEPER'S HANDBOOK

Jeanne K. Posey

Photographs by Robert Nolan

COLLIER BOOKS
A Division of Macmillan Publishing Co., Inc.
New York

COLLIER MACMILLAN PUBLISHERS
London

Macmillan Publishing Co., Inc.
866 Third Avenue, New York, N. Y. 10022
Collier Macmillan Canada, Ltd.

The Horse Keeper's Handbook was published in a hardcover
edition by Winchester Press and is reprinted by agreement.

Library of Congress Cataloging in Publication Data
Posey, Jeanne K.
The horse keeper's handbook.
Includes index.
1.   Horses.   I.   Title.
SF285.3.P67 1975   636.1   75-6971
ISBN 0-02-063550-8

First Collier Books Edition 1975

Printed in the United States of America

Contents

Introduction

MOST OF THE information contained in this book came from practical experience, rather than book learning. Most of what you learn about horses will come from this source also. It is impossible to learn everything you need to know from reading books, because each horse, like each horse owner, is different.

I have attempted in this book to furnish a basic foundation of practical advice on the care of horses. Everything I have suggested has worked for me, and hopefully it will also make your job of learning to care for and handle horses a little easier. However, I strongly suggest that you read other books on horse care too, and get as much practical experience as you can. If the things I have suggested do not work for you, do not hesitate to try someone else's suggestion, or use your own ingenuity. For in the long run, your own judgment, your own experience, and your knowledge of your particular horse will be your best guides; books such as this can do no more than point the way.

Part I

STABLE MANAGEMENT

1

The Stable

THIS BOOK, AND most horse care, begins with the stable. Not that a stable is completely indispensable to the horse's health or survival, of course, for a great many horses and ponies have lived out their whole lives without ever knowing the luxury of a stall of their own. Nonetheless, most modern horse keepers begin with the assumption that their horse will need stabling at least some of the time, and most of them arrange for some kind of stabling before they acquire a horse.

They are right in doing so, too, for most horse care is accomplished in and centers around the stable, even in very mild climates, and a comfortable stall will do much to keep your horse healthy and happy, and help him to be a pleasant ride and an enjoyable companion.

Stables vary considerably in size, quality, comfort, and design. If you are lucky enough to be able to build your own, and can afford to do the job right, you will be able to get plans for and design a neat, well ventilated, well-laid-out little barn that will house your horse or horses both comfortably and attractively.

On the other hand, you may have to make do with what is already there, and that may range from a lean-to to a fancy twelve-stall (or more) horse barn. The usual affair will probably fall somewhere in between. It may be all the things you want it to be, or it may be woefully inadequate. Even so, it can usually be improved to make a suitable home for your horse.

The ideal stable has stalls a minimum of 8 feet by 10 feet, but preferably either 10 by 12 or 12 by 14, with a hard-packed dirt floor. It is well drained, has dutch doors, a high window placed well for good ventilation, sturdy, undrafty walls, and strong latches on the doors. It has no protruding objects inside, and has good drainage around it, a place to cross-tie the horse, and room for feed and tack storage that is clean, dry and relatively warm. It has enough room for feed and hay to keep you from having to run

Homemade, two-stall stable made from scrap lumber. Roof slants to rear for drainage. Stable faces east, is sheltered by large trees. There are no windows but no top doors either; ventilation is through tops of doors.

to the farm supply store every week, and the storage is in such a place that the horse cannot get to it. The ideal stable is dry, fairly warm, and situated with its front in the lee of the prevailing winds. It has a paddock around it so that you can readily turn out the horse in a small area for exercise instead of always having to turn him out into the big pasture, and so you can isolate new or visiting horses from him.

That is what it looks like if it is ideal. If, however, your stable does not match up to these specifications, this book is for you. Horse care can only be as good as the stable. You can be the most kindhearted and diligent person alive, but if your stable is inadequate your horse will be missing what is, to him, the most important part of his care: a comfortable home. And if he is not comfortable, he won't be much of a pleasure to own and to ride. When you get your stable fixed up so that it is comfortable, then you can begin to give that horse good care.

The first problem to discuss is drainage. Many barns now used as stables were not originally intended to house horses, but even some that were suffer equally from poor drainage. Inadequate drainage means more than having to wear hip boots to get to your horse's stall; it means keeping the horse on ground that is almost constantly wet, which is very bad for his feet, not to mention having to clean off his mud-encrusted legs before you can ride. In short, it means keeping him in unhealthy conditions which endanger his most important part: his feet and legs.

If your barn is built in a low area because someone accidentally picked the lowest spot on the farm, you may have to move it. Filling and grading may also solve the problem. Usually, the barn was built on a good spot, but years of rain running off the roof has dug trenches under the eaves that collect water and make a mud pond between you and the doors.

I am a great believer in investing in gutters for stables. They well repay the expense. If you can't bring yourself to put out the extra money, digging drainage ditches may help, and some filling in here and there may be necessary. Find someone who knows something about grading and drainage to look the situation over and give you some advice. Both you and your horse will greatly benefit from it.

Another irritating problem is a stable that is laid out poorly. Sometimes this comes as a result of adding stalls onto a barn without stopping to think about how much trouble it will be to have to feed the horses and clean the stable. The result is the barn that has all the stalls opening on different sides of the stable. This does keep the horses from fighting with one another as they go in and out, but it also develops your leg muscles

Stall built into old tobacco barn. Walls and door are made extra high for horse who jumps out of regular stalls.

excessively as you walk round and round locking horses in, feeding them, etc. If you have a stable built this way, you may be able to cut doors in the stalls to provide access from the feed room to the stalls without having to go outside. This is a great help in rainy weather. If the stable is built in such a way that doing this is impractical, building an overhang around it can help, and spare you from putting on underwater gear to feed in the rain or snow.

Problems with ventilation are probably less common, but they do occur. Barns that are too drafty may be chinked up in various ways, and of course the horses can be blanketed. A greater problem is the barn that is too hot and stuffy in the summer. Stalls with no windows, and stalls located in the back of a barn have a tendency to be hot when doors are closed, causing problems from heat, flies, and dust. The easiest solution to this problem may be to put up stall guards and some sort of barricade across the entrance to the barn so the big doors can be left open to let the breeze circulate through the barn. In addition, a rigid fly spraying schedule should be met, as well as careful removal and disposal of manure.

Wet stalls, which are really a drainage problem, will ruin a horse's feet in short order. The kind of stall that stays wet in the middle should have the floor built up with soil so that moisture drains out. A sprinkling of lime when the stall is cleaned will also help.

Some problems with stable layout are merely inconveniences. For instance, a bucket or manger placed at the back of the stall instead of by the door necessitates walking past the horse's hindquarters to deliver feed, as well as causing extra walking.

If your stable has anything but good, hard-packed dirt for a floor, something should be done. Concrete has all kinds of good points as far as strength of the building and drainage, but it is unsuitable for horses if it is uncovered. It puts a strain on legs and feet, as it has no give to it. Concrete should be covered with a minimum of 18 inches of hard-packed dirt. There is no practical substitute I know of for this cushion. The first foot of it can be small rocks or gravel, but the top 6 to 8 inches should be dirt.

Asphalt flooring can be used, but I would not recommend it for use with horses that are stabled for hours on end, as it too has little give to the feet and legs. It should also be noted that both concrete and asphalt may become slippery when wet by urine.

Wood flooring should be torn out and disposed of. It rots quickly and causes odors and dampness in the stable, and it harbors not only worms, but also rats and other vermin beneath it.

If you are building a stable yourself, or if the one you have was homemade, you may have a stall door that opens the wrong way. Stall doors should always open to the outside of the stall. In case of fire, a horse can break out of the stall if the door opens to the outside, but otherwise he would actually have to break the door to get out. If you want to open the door and the horse wants to come out at the same time, it is much easier if you don't have to push him back to get the door open, and he is less likely to hurt himself getting out of the stall. In addition, a door swinging inward cuts down on usable stall space, and if the floor gets built up with pushed up dirt or manure the door may be impossible to open at all.

This stall doorway is too narrow! Yearling has a close shave coming out; full grown horse would catch hips.

Latches on stall doors should be of some type that you can open easily but the horse cannot. The necessary hardware is well worth the expense and will save endless aggravation when you have an impatient horse at your shoulder. The sliding bar type of latch on doors and gates is practical only if the door is well enough hung so that it doesn't sag. With sliding bars on gates, remember that most of the time you will only have one hand free to manipulate it. Much of the time and effort can be taken out of horse care if simple things like these are taken into account when planning is done.

It is a good idea, if at all possible, to arrange a set of cross-ties in the stable. They are handy, practical, and add to the efficiency of the stable plan. The horse can be cross-tied for grooming, cleaning the feet, shoeing, vet care, etc. Cross-ties should be set at a level about even with the horse's eyes, and at such a length that the horse cannot move his head more than a few inches to either side. They should be short enough so that the chains must be almost taut to fasten onto each side of the halter. A loose tie can be dangerous, as the horse may hook a leg over it, or even catch his nose or mouth in a loop of chain if it is loose. Properly adjusted, cross-ties can keep even a feisty horse under control.

Cross-ties are usually set in an aisle or under an overhanging roof, but they can also be put in the stall. Even if the cross-ties are outside, a single chain tie can be put in a strategic place in the stall to tie the horse for medical attention, etc. and I like to put one in each stall. A chain tie with a heavy snap is handy because it does not require tying knots.

If you put lights in your stable, make sure that all wires are led out of the way and are protected from a curious horse's teeth. Put light switches in the feed room or in the aisle, but not in the stalls. It is not unusual for a horse to learn how to turn on his light, and the added electricity bill probably won't be appreciated. Put the lights high enough so the horse cannot reach them even if he rears. A good place to put light fixtures may be directly over the partition between the stalls, or in the aisle.

Remember that barn lights are a convenience for you, not the horse. They need only be bright enough for you to see your way around. There should be, however, at least one light in the barn that is strong enough for you to see cuts or other injuries, in case they occur at night or have to be treated at night. Also, if you have a foaling box (a stall for a mare to foal in and that you will keep her and the foal in), the light in it should be bright enough for the vet to work by if necessary.

2

Pasture and Fencing

EVEN IF STABLING is good horses also need pasture. At the very least, they should have a place to exercise at liberty, even if it is only a small paddock. Horses that are always confined in stalls and exercised only by being longed or ridden are not only harder to handle than those that are given some freedom every day, but also often develop nervous habits from boredom.

Pasture doesn't mean just a field that turns green in the summer. There is good pasture and bad pasture. The grass in a field might be a foot high, but if it is full of weeds and briars, and is tough and bitter, it will not keep your horses fat and healthy. And even if your pasture does have good grass, it needs to be cared for properly to remain nutritious. In addition, pasture that is used constantly has more worms on it, and horses kept on the same field year round will need to be wormed more often.

Even if your pasture is small, you will get more use out of it if you divide it in two and use half at one time, rotating back and forth twice a year. Plowing under, cultivating and reseeding the unused half will keep the grass nutritious and tasty, and will drastically cut the worm population as well.

Many people, of course, do not have the equipment, or the time, to properly cultivate good pasture, but several alternatives are possible. Even if the grass is very lush and relatively free of weeds, the pasture should be divided. This allows it to reseed itself and improve, rather than deteriorating, as it will if it is grazed constantly. Also, the pasture should be mowed periodically. Grass becomes tough and bitter if it grows over about six inches in height (depending on the type of grass) and mowing helps it to replenish itself. You may be able to find a neighbor with a tractor and "bush hog" to mow it for you.

If you do cultivate and reseed, use a pasture grass recommended by your county agent. He will probably recommend a good volunteer crop.

If your pasture is scanty, weedy, or other-

Poor pasture. Grass is short and sparse, and there are many bare patches.

wise not up to par, do not depend on it to keep your horses fit. Do not hesitate to feed grain and/or hay if necessary—the extra expense will be well worth it to have healthy, usable horses.

The matter of fencing is the second basic consideration involved in pasturage. Barbed wire is obviously unsuitable for horses, although it is fairly widely used in some parts of the country. If barbed wire must be used, the posts should be set closely together (no more than 8 feet apart) and the wire strung tightly. The barbs should be cut down with wire cutters on at least the top strand of wire. Old wire will be considerably less sharp than new.

Whenever possible, however, wire fencing should be replaced with boards, post-and-rail, cable, electric fencing, or woven wire. Fencing should be safe, tight, high enough to keep the horses from wanting to jump out, and low enough so that small ponies and foals cannot roll under it. The highest board should be no less than $3\frac{1}{2}$ feet, and the lowest at about 18 inches. Posts should be set 8 feet apart for board fencing, and no more than 10 feet apart for any kind of fencing.

Gates should be strong, well hung, and easy to open and close for the owner, but not for the horse. The gate should open to the inside of the pasture to make it easier to get in and out, and so that if the horse leans on it and opens it, it will not swing out. "Walk-throughs" can be left at the corners of the fence or next to the gate if desired. If

Poor fencing. Gate originally had a sliding bar fastening, but now has a rope and chain. (Horses had learned to open the sliding bar.)

there are small ponies or foals in the pasture, it is usually wise to hook a chain across these openings.

Pastures are for livestock; keep machinery, automobiles, etc. out.

If electric fencing is used, make sure that the wire has rags tied to it carefully so the horse can see it easily. Sometimes a horse will run right through a lightweight wire fence without even seeing it. Some people use a strand of barbed wire for an electric fence, thinking that the heavier wire is safer, but I do not recommend it. If the horse accidentally touches the electric fence, he may jump in fright, and if he jumps the wrong way and the wire is sharp, he may cut himself.

3

Stable Cleaning

IF THE STABLE is kept dirty the horse will suffer, no matter how fancy or well built the barn is. There are two main reasons for keeping the stable clean. One is the horse's feet. Dirty stalls will cause thrush and other foot problems, which may eventually cause lameness. Dirty conditions also add to the fly problem and make the worm situation worse. In addition to these two practical problems, a dirty stable has an offensive odor, and the horses will be dirty and objectionable also. As any horse owner knows, horses smell wonderful, but dirty horses and a dirty barn aren't pleasant even to the most devout horse lover, and they will definitely not smell good to your neighbors. This is particularly significant if you live in a subdivision, where complaints from surrounding homes may cause the area to be re-zoned to exclude horses entirely.

Stable cleaning, like the rest of stable management, is largely a matter of routine. Stall cleaning is a lot easier if it is done often. If your horse is stabled only at night, or if he goes in and out at will, you may not need to clean thoroughly more than twice a week, but if he spends much time in the stall it must be done daily.

If you use straw for bedding, you will want to fork out and save what clean, dry straw you can salvage. But instead of just picking around and taking out the manure and wet straw, clean the whole stall out, down to the floor. A little garden cart is lightweight and handy to use, and will usually hold enough waste to clean several stalls. After the floor is cleared of all manure and bedding, rake it level. You may want to shift some of the dirt around to fill in low spots, such as where the horse paws at the feed box, for instance. After it is raked and level, sprinkle lime lightly on the damp spots, and let the stall air out for a while. Depending on how damp the stall is, you may want to leave it just while you do the other stalls, or you may have to wait several hours for it to get good and dry. Leave the door open and put up a stall guard if it is necessary to keep the horse out.

After the floor has aired, bed the stall again, using the straw that you saved plus enough fresh straw to cover the floor. Avoid putting the horse into a wet or damp stall. If the stall floor takes an unusually long time to dry, or if it stays wet in some places all of the time, it may need to be releveled or built up to improve drainage.

If you use sawdust for bedding, one of the new shovels made specially for this purpose may be handy. Otherwise, rake and shovel up droppings, and rake damp places down so that the wet sawdust is exposed to the air. Then air the stall until dry. Standing in wet bedding will cause thrush to develop quickly or cause it to thrive if it is already present. In addition, wet conditions will make a horse's hooves soft and weak generally.

It is also wise to spray a disinfectant on the walls and floors of the barn periodically, and sweeping cobwebs and dirt off the walls once in a while will cut down on dust.

Once the stall is cleaned, you will have the cartful of used bedding and manure to dispose of. Pick a spot as far away from the stable as is at all convenient, but never in the pasture, to make your manure pile. Then periodically dump the whole pile somewhere, even if you have to take it to the dump. Do not spread it on ground that will be used for pasture within a year. Put it on the garden, on the lawn, give it to your neighbors, sell it to mushroom growers—anything, but don't just let it pile up and up. Manure is a favorite breeding place for flies and worms. It doesn't accomplish much to get it out of the barn and then leave it on the pasture where the horses can roll in it. If you have a farm and use a manure spreader, you may want to park the spreader near the barn and empty things directly into it, or if you use a wagon, you can load directly onto it.

When you have finished cleaning the stalls, don't forget to put the tools away, including the cart. If possible, keep the cart in the stable in an extra stall, or somewhere that the horses won't trip over it. Otherwise lean it up against the side of the stable on a side that doesn't get much traffic. Keep the pitchfork, shovel and rake in the feed room, or otherwise out of both the horse's way and yours.

In most climates flies are a source of aggravation and problems in the summer. Using ear nets and fly sheets may be helpful, as can the various patented fly-

catching devices, but probably the best solution is to keep a clean stable and to use fly
repellent. There are several excellent repellents for use in the stable, and they should
be used often, according to the directions
on the label, of course.

There are also good repellents for use on
the horse, but I would not recommend
using them constantly. Fly repellents are
relatively expensive, and while they are not
harmful to the horse's skin when used mod-
erately, it may be asking for trouble to use
them too freely. Put some around the face,
ears and neck of the horse when you ride,
following the directions on the can, but as
far as the pasture and stable are concerned,
remember that horses have been fighting
flies for centuries, and there is no reason to
suppose they cannot continue to do so suc-
cessfully. If, however, a horse has cuts or
sores that draw flies, use repellent around
these areas to help keep them away.

4

Feeding

EVERY BOOK ON horse care ever written has its chapter or chapters on feeding. You can get information on kinds of feeds, how much of what kind to feed, how much protein, carbohydrates, fats, etc., each type of grain has, and what kinds of minerals are available. I feel that a scientific explanation of the food values of the various kinds of feeds is superfluous here, and probably beyond the average reader's interest anyway. Sometimes too many facts tend to confuse the reader rather than to enlighten him; the only practical way to look at the business of what and how much to feed is the simple way.

First, it is important to remember that the horse was originally a grazing animal. He has a small stomach in relation to his body size, and is designed to eat small amounts of food fairly constantly. When horses are out on pasture you will notice that they graze all day, off and on, keeping more or less full all the time.

However, a horse that is kept on pasture only part of the time, or not at all, cannot practically obtain a steady stream of food all day. Moreover, the food we use as a substitute for natural grasses is grain, and since grain is a concentrate the horse eats less of it than he would grass. Thus a stabled horse needs both hay and grain to provide the same diet that he would get on good pasture.

Of equal importance to food in a horse's diet is water. A horse must have an adequate supply of clean, fresh water in order to stay in good health. A horse deprived of water will lose weight and become unthrifty. Without sufficient water he cannot digest his food properly, and may lose weight even with increased food. Severe dehydration can cause drastic digestive disturbances, and eventually death.

The water bucket or other container in the stall should be raised to about chest level on the horse so that dirt can't collect in it, and should be put close to the door for convenience in filling. It should be removable for cleaning. It should be rinsed out between fillings, and thoroughly cleaned about once a week. The water bucket should be kept full whenever the horse is in the stall.

Water containers in paddocks and pastures should also be easy to clean. Many people use an old bathtub, which is excellent, provided it is cleaned regularly. (Some bathtubs are very heavy; be sure that the plug is readily removable.) If the tub is a modern one with one sharp edge designed to fit the wall of the house, make sure this edge is placed against the fence, away from the horse's legs, for many horses have a tendency to paw at the water container.

Put the water trough somewhere where it is shady in summer, but preferably not under a tree. (Up against a building, for instance, on the east side, as the morning sun is not as hot as the afternoon.) Remember to check for ice in the winter, and break it up if necessary, and check the water often in summer, as the horses will tend to drink more.

It is not necessary to heat the water in winter or cool it in the summer, as the horses will drink it at any temperature. However, if the horse is hot from exertion, water him in slow stages, a little at a time, to prevent his body temperature from dropping too rapidly. Do not ride the horse hard right after he has had a long drink, and wait a full hour after feeding before working the horse above a walk. Founder or colic can easily occur if these warnings are ignored.

Horses also need a constant source of salt in their diets. Salt provides the important service of maintaining the acidity level in the horse's body, and a lack of it will interfere with digestion and cause the horse to become unthrifty. As long as the horse is receiving enough water, whatever excess salt he may be receiving will be eliminated in the urine. Because of the variation in salt content in different areas of soil, and the differences in the amount of salt found in different grasses and feeds, it is difficult to establish just how much salt a horse needs to be fed. Therefore an easy method of feeding salt is to give the horse free choice, allowing him to eat as much or as little as he wants. This can best be done by providing the horse with a salt block, placed either in the pasture or in the stall. Salt blocks come plain, or with minerals. Ask your county agent to test your soil for trace minerals to determine whether your horse needs mineral salt.

Another way to feed salt is to put loose

salt in the feed daily. The average horse should probably get from 6 to 8 ounces of table salt in this manner daily.

Horses should be provided with natural grass if it is possible. A horse can be sustained on one acre of actual pasture, not including trees and cover. This means that for every horse you pasture, you will need at least one full acre of good natural grass to keep him fat without having to supply extra feed. However, unless you live in a climate where the grass supply stays constant throughout the year, the grass will dry up and diminish in the winter, and extra feed must be supplied during these months.

In addition, if you have your horse on a riding program, you will probably find that grass will not provide enough calories to keep him fit, and that you will have to add grain and possibly some hay to his diet. There is a world of difference between keeping a horse alive and keeping him fat. If you can see your horse's ribs, if his hindquarters tend to peak in the middle and are not fairly rounded, if his neck is hollowed out, and if his backbone seems quite pronounced, he is definitely too thin. Variations in conformation make some horses seem more angular and lean than others, but generally a horse should be well-rounded. Because of the differences in individuals, what will keep a grade horse fat may starve a Thoroughbred. If your horse is thin, but otherwise healthy, you're not feeding him enough, no matter how much or how little your neighbor may be feeding his horse. It's just like it is with people.

If you have a large, lush pasture and a few horses, they will probably stay fat in the summer at least, and have to be fed some hay and grain in the winter. Differences in pasture make a difference, however. Not all grass is nutritious enough to keep a working horse fit, even though it may be available in ample supplies. Looking at the horse is the best way to tell if his pasture is adequate.

A horse that is not getting pasture, or that is pastured on little or no actual grass, must be fed both hay and grain. Very small ponies may do well on hay only, but larger ponies and horses need grain. A horse needs both the roughage of hay and the concentrated nutrients of grain to substitute for his natural diet. A horse that is getting all hay and no grain will usually develop a "hay belly," because his digestive system cannot handle enough roughage to provide the necessary nutrients to keep him fat.

The kind of hay you use will depend on what is available in your area. In my locale (Southern Maryland), for instance, clover, timothy and lespedeza are grown, while alfalfa is hard to get except in very large quantities from farther north.

Whatever type of hay you use, it must be fresh smelling, clean, free of weeds, mold or dust, and must be cured properly. Often hay is rendered virtually worthless by incorrect curing. Hay should be at least faintly green in color, and lespedeza and alfalfa particularly should be very green. Hay that is a dull brown in color may have been over-cured, and at any rate its food value is very small. Lespedeza and clover are higher in protein than timothy hay, but timothy is generally cleaner, less weedy, and easier to cure. In our area lespedeza has a tendency to be very weedy, and it is harder to find it properly cured. Lespedeza also may have a tendency to be moldy in the center of the bale, due to the heat it produces while curing, and when buying it may be wise to break open a bale or two and check it. Often you can find a mixture of timothy and other grasses that makes a green, tasty hay. Do not buy hay that is more than six months old, and do not buy any that has any evidence of having had rats in it. Hay with old, discolored baling string or wire should be suspected.

It is usually cheaper to get good hay if you find a farmer who will sell it off the field. This way you know the hay is fresh and you can pick and choose the bales you want. If you are looking at lespedeza, lift each bale and feel the ground under it. If the ground is unusually warm, it may mean that the hay is still curing, and may have been baled undercured. This means several things: if fed before the curing process is finished, the hay will cause colic, while if stored in a closed barn the heat given off during curing may cause a fire. In addition, the bales will be likely to mold in the middle.

It is a good rule not to feed hay right out of the field, anyway; give it a week or two to be safe. (Use up your older hay while the new hay is curing.) When you get hay out of a field, particularly with lespedeza, walk around and heft several bales. Then pick bales that are neither very much lighter or heavier than most of the ones you have checked. If you are paying by the bale, extra light bales are uneconomical; by the ton they will take up more storage space. Extra heavy bales may mean that the bale is wet on the inside or that it is packed so tightly that it will become moldy on the inside.

If you have only one or two horses, do not buy more hay than you can use up in a few months, even if you can get a much cheaper price. Find a neighbor to share it with you so that you don't end up with old hay on your hands. Also, do not buy more hay than you can store properly. Covering it with a tarp and leaving it out in the open will eventually ruin it, and then you won't have saved anything by getting it cheap. Bad hay makes horses sick, and vet bills are not cheap, as everyone knows.

Unless the ground is muddy there is no reason why hay cannot be fed off the ground outside the stable. In the stall, however, feeding off the floor has several disadvantages. The horse is likely to soil the hay or carry it around until he walks on it. (Outside he has room enough to stay out of it.) Also, it will get mixed up with the bedding, encouraging the horse to eat his bedding. A wooden manger can be used for hay, if the stall is large enough to accommodate it. This keeps the hay off the floor but down at a level where it won't get in the horse's eyes. The manger should be built so the

Wooden manger in stall with feed box. Boards do not reach floor so they won't rot, and do not quite reach wall, leaving a space for small particles of hay to drop through. (There is a horizontal bottom inside.)

horse cannot roll under it and get caught.
Another alternative is the hay rack, which can be made of metal or wood, or a hay net. A rack or net must be hung high enough to

insure that the horse cannot get a hoof hung in it if he should paw at it, which means that it is also high enough to get dirt and chaff in the horse's eyes as he pulls the hay out. A hay rack or net is also harder for a small person to fill. If a rack is used, it should be placed in the opposite corner of the stall from the water bucket, to keep dust and hay from getting in the water.

Sometimes it is possible to get old hay very cheap, or even free. If you are tempted to do this, use it for only one purpose: spread it on fields not used for pasture this year, or use it for mulch for your garden. Do NOT use it for feed, or for bedding, or put it anywhere that horses can get to it. No matter how old or how bad hay is, horses will probably eat it. At best, old hay is dusty and useless; at worst, it may be poisonous.

The type of grain you feed your horses may depend on how many horses you have and the type of use you get out of them. If you have quite a few horses you may feel it is cheaper to mix your own feed, rather than buying a commercial mix. Commercial mixes, while nutritionally complete, have a fairly high percentage of chaff in them, which raises their cost and lowers their food value per pound.

You will want your horse to get a mix of oats (crimped or whole), whole or cracked corn, linseed meal (or soybean meal), and possibly also cracked barley or bran. You may want to add vitamin supplements to this, depending on whether or not you ride your horses a lot, or whether you have young stock. (See chapter on Care of Very Young or Very Old Horses.)

You can buy commercial sweet feed, which includes all of the above, plus beet pulp, molasses, and vitamins and minerals. Beet pulp adds bulk and some food value to

Two types of prepared feed: on the left is sweet feed, on the right a pelleted feed especially for foals. All-in-One pellets are larger than these.

the grain; molasses improves the pala-
tability and keeps the grain from being
dusty. When buying sweet feed mixes, compare the labels on several brands and types
within a brand to determine which is more
economical, and which mixtures have the
highest food value per pound.

In addition to sweet feeds, there are also
feeds on the market which are known as
"All-in-One" feeds. These come in pellet
form and have alfalfa meal added which
provides the nutrients of hay in the diet.
Thus you can give the horse the same bal-
anced diet of hay and grain, without having
to store all that hay. The disadvantage of
this is that the pellets do not provide the
roughage that hay does. As the digestive
system of the horse is designed for
roughage, digestive disorders may arise
from its lack. Also, hay gives the horse
something to do during the time he is in the
stall; without it, he may develop nervous
habits such as cribbing and weaving. All-in-
One feeds are useful as a single feed for
short periods of time on camping trips or in
areas where hay is not available. It is also of
great value when the only hay available is
of poor nutritional value, and added to the
regular diet it is very useful for fattening a
horse up.

Grain supplies energy to the horse, as well as providing protein, vitamins and minerals. Oats are fairly high in protein, spoil less quickly than most grains, and are easily digestible. However, some horses, particularly those that bolt their food, may choke on whole oats, as they are smooth and have a tendency to pack when wet by saliva. Crimped oats may be safer to feed a horse that tends to choke, may be easier to digest for some horses, and are about 5% higher in food value than whole oats.

Corn supplies carbohydrates to the diet and is useful in fattening up horses, as it is high in calories. Added to the diet in winter, it helps maintain a layer of fat through cold weather. However, horses with low metabolisms, horses with draft blood or pony blood, and particularly small ponies tend to become overfat and overly energetic if fed corn.

There is a lot of discussion about which feeds are better, and which you should use, but my advice is this: Feed your horse "horse feed," in the amounts recommended (approx. 10 lbs of grain per day for each 1000 lbs. of body weight, figuring that a 15.2 hand horse will weigh about 1000 lbs) and then adjust the amount as your horse needs. Remember to weigh out whatever mea-

suring vehicle you use with the feed you
are using, for while a two-pound coffee can
of oats weighs about two pounds, the same
amount of sweet feed will weigh more. Regular horse feed should be satisfactory for
your horse, provided that he is getting good
hay, adequate water and salt.

If you have him on a heavy work schedule, if he is very young, or if you have a
mare in foal, he or she may need a vitamin
supplement as well. If you want your horse
to have a sleek show coat, or if he is recov-
ering from an illness and has lost the
bloom to his coat, or if you are trying to
bring a thin horse up in condition, you may
want to give a vitamin-mineral supplement
in addition to the regular feed. There are a
number of supplements on the market available at feed stores and tack stores, and your
vet may have a favorite he would recommend. Many times a supplement means the
difference between a "just average" horse,
and the shining, glowing kind of health that
makes people admire you for the way you
care for your animals, and that can turn an
ordinary horse into a keen, happy pleasure
to ride. Coat conditioners are available for
the show coat, too.

Some horses stay fat on practically

nothing, and small ponies in particular are noted for being "easy keepers." On the other hand, some horses eat more than the usual amounts and never seem to get fat. One of the ways to help a horse be an easy keeper is to feed him on a rigid schedule. Tests have been run that prove that it takes less feed to maintain a horse's weight if the horse is fed within an hour of the same times every day, and in the same place every feeding. Maintaining a schedule, and feeding at least twice a day can make as much as three or four pounds of grain difference per day in the amount of feed your horse needs.

Pick a time of day that you know you can always be available to feed. Before work in the morning, and as late as ten o'clock at night, if that is the only time you are sure you will always be there. The horse doesn't care if it is late at night, just as long as it is the same time each night. If you always come straight home from work, you can schedule it then.

Feeding in the same place is also part of the routine. One of the reasons a horse stays fat on less feed with regular feeding is that he gets attuned to eating at a certain time and frets if the feed is late. It upsets his habits if things are changed, and horses are creatures of habit. It also excites him unnecessarily if the feeding place is moved, and feeding in the same place every day is more convenient for you, too. Once the horse is used to being fed in one spot, you won't have to lead him to it, he will go there automatically.

Ideally, you will have a separate stall for each horse, and will shut each horse in his stall to feed him. However, if you have the open shelter type of barn, you have somehow to separate the horses during meals. If you have two paddocks, you can put one horse in each, or you may have to tie them apart. But even if your horses all eat the same amount of feed, it is not wise to leave them loose together while they are eating. Not only will they probably fight, but the fatter, more aggressive horse will get more than his share, while the more timid horses will get less than they should. If you do not have the time to tie them up and then come back to turn them loose, put up enough fences or stalls to keep them apart.

If you do tie your horses to separate them, make sure that they are far enough apart so they cannot kick each other, and put them far enough apart so they don't worry each

Always separate horses when feeding them; other-wise, the larger horse will get all the feed.

other. Many horses will bolt their feed be-cause they are afraid that another horse may come over and chase them away. They are not necessarily smart enough to know that no one can get loose and get them.

Do not feed grain off the ground, for the horse will eat a lot of dirt trying to get the last few grains. Outside, a bucket or feed box can be set on the ground, as the horse will move off when finished, although it is better to fasten it on a fence or building to keep the horse from tipping it over. In the stall, the container should always be fastened to the wall so the horse cannot step in it or soil it.

If your horse dribbles his grain over the sides of the bucket, it may help to set the bucket in a corner with a large lip around it (it can be made of plywood), or to put a sack or board under the bucket to catch the dropped feed.

If your horse has a tendency to bolt his food, putting one of those two-pound salt blocks or a few large rocks in his feed box may help to slow him down. If necessary, feed him in 4 or 5 smaller feedings per day to keep him from choking. A bolter will often learn to slow down by himself eventually if he is fed in quiet surroundings with no other horses in sight.

Unless it is necessary, do not stay in your horse's stall while he is eating. Save grooming and other chores until later whenever possible; leave him alone during meals. Some horses react very violently to being disturbed while eating, and there is no reason to aggravate a horse in the middle of dinner. It only disrupts his digestion.

From time to time there have been great controversies about the best order for feeding water, hay and grain. (I just named them in the usually recommended order.) However, unless a horse is starving, or has been deprived of water, there is little danger in feeding in an order other than the one above. If the horse has been without water all day, then I would recommend giving him water first, as it is the most important element in his diet. Of course, good stable management gives the horse free choice of water, so he should never come to dinner thirsty.

If you put all three items in the stall, and then turn the horse loose, most horses will naturally drink first. Unless the horse is starving, it will not make much difference whether the grain or hay comes first, and in the case of building up a starving animal, the grain given at first is in very small amounts. Most horses will eat their grain first, then wait a while and eat their hay slowly, making it last all night.

If the horse is in the stall already, I feed in the recommended order mainly out of convenience. I fill the water bucket (if necessary) first, throw in the hay to keep the horse from getting impatient, and then feed the grain.

If you have been riding your horse regularly, and for some reason you suddenly have to take him out of work, do not continue to give him a full grain ration. Cut his grain ration a third to a half when work slacks off or stops, to prevent him from foundering. It will also keep him from becoming unmanageably energetic from being fed too much grain with too little work. Any time you stop riding a horse that is kept in a stall, make sure that you longe him or turn him out for exercise at least once a day. Horses need daily exercise, even if it is only a run around the paddock. Stable vices begin with boredom, and founder and other ailments can be caused by inactive horses that are getting too much feed.

If you decide to change to a different kind of feed, make the transition gradually. When you decide a horse is too thin, don't double his grain all at once. Add a pound or two for a week at a time, until the desired level is reached. If you are changing types of grains, blend in a pound or two of the new kind for a week, then go half and half, then three-fourths, then complete. Give the horse a chance to get used to the new feed.

If you have pasture in the summer, but have to grain all winter, make the changes in spring and fall gradually, too. In the fall, when the grass begins to give out, start small rations of grain while there is grass, and gradually increase the grain as needed. In the spring, don't turn the horse out to a pasture full of new grass indiscriminately. Phase the grass in and the grain out over a period of several weeks, at first allowing the horse only an hour or two on the grass at a time. New grass causes colic easily, and also sometimes produces diarrhea, and a horse cannot make the transition from grain to grass quickly.

If there are fruit trees in your pasture, either keep the horses away from the green fruit, or pick it up so they don't colic on it. If you have only one or two trees and a lot of horses, you may not have a problem, but one horse and one tree that bears well could be disastrous.

5

Handling in the Stable

ALMOST THE FIRST thing you do with a horse when you get him home and something that you will do countless times with any horse, is to put him in his stall. Oh, you say, that's simple, you just open the door and let him go in. But what if he doesn't want to go in? What if he catches his hip on the door and hurts himself? And what if he turns around and heads the other way?

Even if your horse is dependably manageable in hand, it is a good idea to always go into the stall with him, instead of turning him loose at the door. If your stall door opens on your right, open it to at least a ninety degree angle to the wall, and lead the horse in with you from your usual position on his left. This way, you can let the horse swing around you as you close the door, keeping between him and the door.

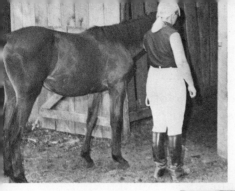

*Putting horse in the stall (stall door opens to left):
Stand at right shoulder and walk in. Then let horse
move past you into stall so that you block the door.*

*The wrong way to put the horse into his stall. What if
he kicks?*

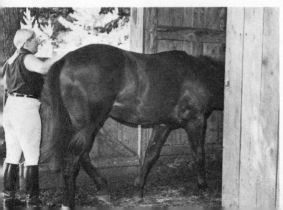

Always keep the horse between you and the wall, so you are closest to the door. Some horses have a disconcerting way of pinning you to the wall with their hindquarters, which puts them in a position to kick you, and you in no position at all! If the door opens to your left, get on the right side of the horse to lead him in, again keeping between him and the door. This is one of the reasons for teaching your horse to lead from the right as well as the left.

It is a good idea to close the door before you let go of the horse, even if he is dependable about staying in. A child always keeps hold of the horse until the door is closed, since he is less able to control the horse than an adult. Keeping hold of the halter or shank gives that much more bargaining power to the handler.

If children are helping with the horse care, it is a good idea to put a latch on the inside of the stall door, so that they can fasten the door from the inside without having to reach over the door.

Haltering a horse may be a difficult thing for a child to do, and it is often unnecessarily hard for anyone. Usually the hardest part of it is getting the horse to stand still. The best method, again, is the simplest.

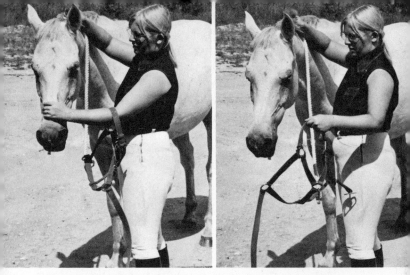

Haltering the horse: Hold the horse with your right hand on the mane behind the ears, carrying the halter over your left arm. Slide the noseband of the halter down to your left hand.

Bring the noseband up and push the loose end of the crownpiece over the head with your right hand, and then buckle it, using both hands.

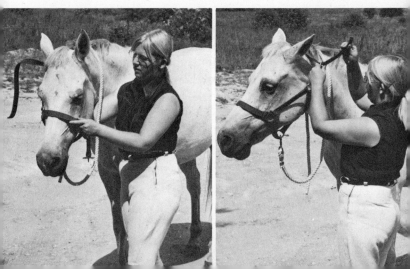

With the crownpiece (the part that goes over the ears) unbuckled, loop the noseband of the halter over your left arm. With your right hand, grasp the horse by the mane just behind his ears. Hold onto his nose just above the nostrils with your left hand. This gives you two handles to hold in case the horse tries to move. When the horse is standing still, let go with your left hand and let the halter drop to your hand. Slide your hand over the horse's nose so that the noseband is in place, pulling it up higher than it will rest when the halter is buckled. Using your left hand now to hold the horse, put your right hand under his neck and pull the crownpiece up, letting it fall over the horse's neck behind his ears. Then use your left hand to bring the near side of the halter up to buckle, using both hands now. You now have both hands on the halter in case the horse tries to move.

If the horse is prone to backing away from you, you can back him into a corner so he cannot move away. If he tries to move forward, try walking him into a corner or against the fence to halter him. You may want to practice haltering in the stall until your technique is smooth and rapid.

It is sensible to leave the halter on the

horse while he is in the stall or left in a small paddock for an hour or so. It makes him easier to catch and hold on to. But what about when you turn him out to pasture?

It might seem natural to turn the horse out with a halter on, to make him easier to catch, but leaving the halter on a horse at pasture can be dangerous. Your horse may go for ten years wearing a halter without mishap, but the tenth year he may get it caught on something and break his leg or neck. This is particularly true of nylon halters, which are unbreakable. And a nice old leather halter which you think would surely break under stress may be surprisingly strong, as I found out once. I left one on a mare that was hard to catch, thinking that since the halter was both old and cheaply made, it would surely fall apart at the least provocation. It put a nasty gouge in that mare's cheek, taught me a lesson, and never did break!

Halters are meant to be a convenience for leading and tying horses, not as a piece of clothing to be worn night and day. They should be taken off when the horse is turned out in the pasture. (Even if the horse never gets hung up by it, he is liable to lose it.)

But what of the horse that is very hard to catch? Or the kind that takes off before you can get the halter on him once you do catch him? Isn't it worth the risk to be able to catch him more quickly? This may depend on the particular horse. Some horses are much easier to catch if they do have a halter on, since they realize that they can't get away as easily. You may want to turn this type of horse out in a soft rope halter. The best solution to the problem, however, is to take the time to teach the horse to stand for haltering and to catch easily. Put the horse in a small paddock and approach him with a handful or two of grain in a bucket. Walk up to his head, gently swishing the bucket so he can hear the grain, and hold it so he can see it when you get close. Be patient. If he moves away, either stop and stand until he finally comes up to you, or keep moving to his head until he stops and stands. Practice catching him in this small enclosure until he comes right up to you, or at least stands until you catch him, and then work up to a larger pen.

While you are teaching him to be caught, don't ride him right after you catch him. Catch him to groom him, feed him, or just turn him out again. Try to plan riding so you take him out of the stall to ride instead of catching him out of the field for a while. Teach him to associate being caught with something good: always give him a treat for being caught, although not from your hand as it encourages nipping. And of course, make his riding time as pleasant as possible. In short, make him like to be caught.

When you do leave a halter on a horse, whether he is in a stall or a paddock, or out at pasture with a rope halter, make sure that it is adjusted so that the noseband is not too loose. Even a horse in a stall could get a foot caught in a loose halter. This is especially true during fly season. Do not be tempted to turn a foal out with a halter, unless it is where you can supervise. Never turn a foal out for even a short while with a halter that is too big for it, on the grounds that it will grow into it, for foals, being especially playful and having small feet, are especially prone to accidents with halters. And young legs are particularly easy to injure.

You will probably have occasion many times to tie your horse for short periods of time. Cross-ties are very handy, and when available should be used whenever possible, as they are safer for both the horse and the owner. It is wise to use a nylon halter, or a very sturdy leather one, to tie the horse with. If you do not have a strong halter, or if you are not sure that the horse will tie without fighting, you may want to put a rope around the neck in a non-slip knot and run it through the halter and tie.

Never tie a horse by the bridle, for not only will it break easily, but the horse might hurt his mouth if he tries to break loose, making him shy of the bridle as well as of being tied. Do not tie a horse with just a rope around the neck as he may turn around and get it tangled about his head or nose. A horse cross-tied with a nylon halter and strong cross-ties cannot get loose even if he fights. Remember, however, that a halter is only as strong as the hardware it is put together with, so check to make sure it is strong and in good condition.

What if cross-ties are unavailable? If your horse is dependable about being tied, and you are going to be around him, you can tie him with a rope or leather lead line. Tie him to something sturdy. If you tie him to a fence, use a post, not a board. Never tie a horse to a wire fence, or near one. Do not tie a horse to a car, particularly not to a door handle. It is also not a good idea to tie a horse to the back of a pickup truck, as he might rear and injure his front legs on the bed, not to mention denting up the truck. If you tie the horse to a horse trailer, tie him midway up one side (many have rings made for this). Never tie him to the trailer hitch, as it is both too low, and dangerous, as he may try to step over it. Do not tie him at the back of an open trailer as he may try to go into the trailer, get caught by the rope, and panic trying to get out again.

A sturdy tree is handy to tie to, although if it is your wife's prize fruit tree she will not appreciate it if the horse rubs all the bark

Horse tied too low. The unnatural angle makes him feel like fighting.

Horse tied too long. He can easily step over rope and become entangled.

off. If you tie the horse to a tree, remember that he will probably try to walk around it, so don't use one that is too close to a fence or building. Do not tie a horse to a gate, as he may pull it out of alignment if he fights. A gate post is all right. If you tie him in a building, such as a garage (for shoeing when it's raining, etc.), make sure that the ceiling is high enough that he cannot hit his head if he rears.

Tie the horse with something that is

strong, that doesn't stretch, that unties easily even if pulled tight, and that is not abrasive enough to cause a burn if the horse gets it wrapped around a leg. Nylon "Samson" cord is good for this purpose, as is the kind of rope used to moor boats. Remember that horses have a tendency to panic when caught in close quarters, particularly if their head is confined. Never assume that a horse will stop fighting a rope before he hurts himself; horses have broken their legs and necks trying to get untangled from ropes.

Tie the horse short enough so that he

Quick release knot. Sticking the free end back through the loop would prevent the horse from pulling the free end and untying himself.

cannot get his front leg over the rope, and tie the knot at a level with his withers, or level with his nose when he is standing normally. Don't tie it above his head, as this unnatural position may make him more likely to try to get away. Don't tie him so short that he can't move at all, as this may make him panic. Almost any horse will fight if the rope gets over his neck, or if his head gets caught in any way. Never stake a horse out on a long rope unless you are going to stand there and watch him closely. Some horses are smart enough not to fight when a rope gets tangled around their legs, but not many. Rope burns can do permanent injury as well as putting the horse out of commission for a while. Just recently a friend of mine had to have a horse destroyed from an injury resulting from a stake rope caught around its hind legs.

6

Problems in the Stable

PROBLEMS IN THE stable fall into two categories: things that just happen, and bad habits or vices that the horse picks up. Neglecting to correct problems as they arise may lead to vices if the horse is allowed to make a habit of doing something wrong. Some problems occur when there are several horses and the owner cannot handle all of them at once.

What happens, for instance, if the horse gets out? In the daytime, when you can see him and he can see you, you can get a bucket with a little feed in it and go after him quickly, and he will probably come right up to you. If he has no halter on, you may find it handy to take a rope and slip it around his neck, if you have only a short way to lead him. Or you can make an emergency halter out of the lead rope.

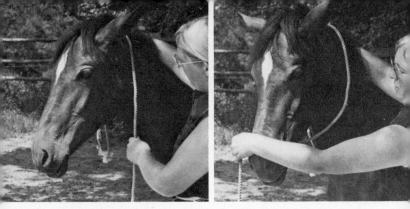

Making an emergency halter from a lead shank, first method: 1. place short end of rope over neck. 2. Loop long end over nose from right side to left.

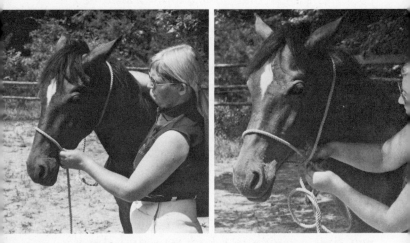

3. Tighten nose loop until fairly snug. 4. Push rope end back under chin, thus making half-hitch over the nose.

There are various ways to do this, but one of the simplest is to put the rope over the horse's neck so there is more rope on the opposite side than on the near, and then make a half-hitch over the horse's nose with the end of the rope, holding both ends under the chin. (See illustration.) This gives control both by pulling on the nose and the neck at the same time. This trick may also come in handy with a horse that is hard to catch in the field. You can first tie the rope around your waist like a belt, so the horse cannot tell you have it. Of course, if your horse is reliable about being caught, you can take your halter.

If it is dark when your horse gets out, don't panic. Chances are that he will not go far very quickly in the dark, even though he

5. Tighten nose loop again. 6. Halter can be held in one hand, putting pressure on both nose and neck of horse.

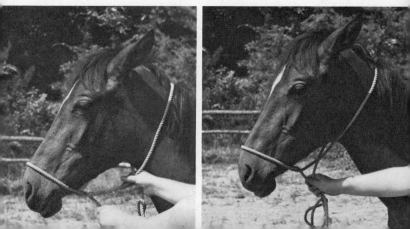

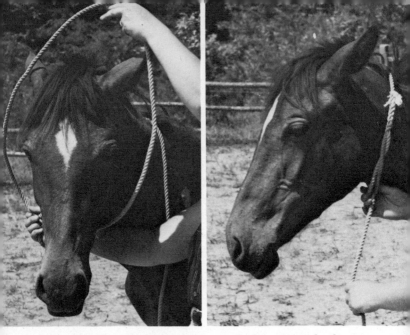

Another form of emergency halter: 1. Make loop in rope and slip over horse's head. 2. Tighten it gently around the throttle.

3. Make another loop over the nose from left to right. 4. Thread loose end through the neck loop.

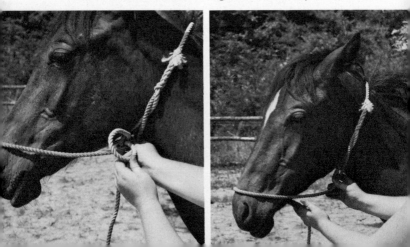

can see better than you can. The first thing
to do is to get your bucket of grain and a
rope, and start calling and talking to him.
Do not take a flashlight, as its beam may
frighten him. Your eyes will gradually get
used to the darkness, and if you listen carefully you will probably be able to hear
him when you get close, even if you can't
see him. Horses make surprisingly loud
crunching noises when they chew and walk
around. Move slowly, keep talking, and
gently shake the bucket so the few handfuls
of grain in it rustle.

When you see or feel or hear the horse at
the bucket, slowly slip the rope around his
neck (or grasp his halter), talking constantly.
Then lead him slowly back to the barn. You

5. *Completed halter gives you only one rope to hold
and is more secure.* 6. *To remove, simply loosen rope
and drop nose loop, pulling it back through neck
loop. Then loosen and remove neck loop.*

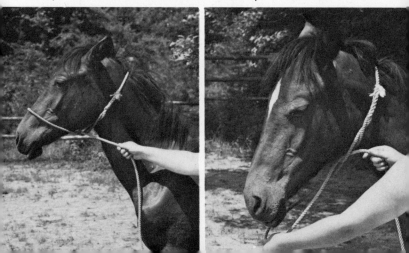

will probably find it is easier to get him to follow you if you carry the bucket with you, and you won't forget and leave it out.

If you have several horses and they get out, remember that they have a strong herding instinct, and that if you catch the leader the others will usually follow him back to the barn. If you're not sure which one is the leader, try to catch the bossiest, most aggressive one, the oldest mare, or the horse that has been on the place the longest, as this type is usually the herd leader. If you cannot catch him, try another, even if you have to catch each one separately. Do not try to herd the whole bunch if you are alone. When you catch one of the horses, put him in a stall. If you just put him back in the pasture, he will try to get out when you let the next one in.

If you have help, you may be able to slowly herd the group back into the pasture or into a paddock, but unless you have at least three people this may be difficult. If you have trouble herding them, or if there are only two of you, you would probably be better off catching them one by one. Do not try to herd them from horseback unless you have a calm, reliable horse and have practiced it before. Usually all you will accomplish is to get the whole herd running. If you herd on foot, try to keep them at a walk, even if it is slow. Lock any dogs up, as they will surely stir things up.

If you live back from the highway and your horses are out but still on your property, you may be able to wait an hour or so, keeping an eye on them, as they are always more likely to want to go home after being out for a while. Sometimes walking by with a bucket will entice them to follow you into the pasture or stall for a treat.

If your horses have gotten out because of a weak spot in the fence, be forewarned that they will test the entire fence line looking for places to get out. While you are fixing one spot, walk the whole line and patch any other weak spots while you are out anyway.

If the horse or horses got out because they figured out how to open the gate, an entirely different type of gate latch may be necessary, or reinforcing whatever latch is there with a chain or rope. Some horses are particularly ingenious at opening latches; in fact, we once had a horse that could open an eye snap. Most horses can learn to untie knots with ease, which is one reason a chain with a stiff snap is often the best fastener.

Sometimes in even the most carefully run

stables, a horse will get into the feed room. If you find your horse with his nose in the feed bin, again, don't panic. Try to determine how much grain he actually ate. If it is more than a normal feeding for him, or if you even suspect that it might be, you should probably assume that he will get colic, or possibly founder, even though he may not.

Look the horse over. Lead him around a little. If he seems unusually sluggish, is reluctant to move, if he has an anxious expression, seems uncomfortable, or nips at his belly or sides, he is probably getting sick. If this is the case, then he may get over it in a few minutes, or it may take a few hours.

If you think the horse may be feeling sick, put him in a stall or paddock with no food or water, and watch him. Do not let him roll or lie down. If it is winter, put a blanket on him and keep him out of drafts. Don't turn him out into a large pasture, and don't just put him in his stall and forget him. Many people recommend walking a horse that has colic or possibly colic, but it is unnecessary unless you have to do it to keep the horse from lying down. Consult the chapter on illnesses for care if the horse shows definite signs of colic or founder.

If the horse seems all right, give him a little water (not more than half a bucket) and keep an eye on him for another few hours. Skip the next regular feeding of grain, and give only a little hay (one or two thin flakes).

If the horse gets out into a corn or wheat field, or onto lush grass when he is not used to it, watch him very carefully. If he becomes sick from this kind of feeding, it may be more serious. Watch for distension of the abdomen from gas. If the horse swells in the hollow just in front of the hip, call the vet immediately. Keep the horse warm and quiet and do not walk him, and do not drench him with a home remedy. This kind of colic (flatulent colic) is caused by gas in the stomach and intestines, and can be fatal.

Even if the horse does not get sick, give him twenty-four hours before returning to regular feeding and work schedules. If he does get sick, give him twenty-four hours from the time of recovery.

What happens if two horses get in the same stall and start fighting? Usually the problem can be left to resolve itself, a few kicks being exchanged and one horse coming back out rapidly. But occasionally one horse will corner another and kick it so hard that there is real danger to the cornered

horse, and you have to do something. DO
NOT run in and try to grab one of the
horses! In fact, don't go in at all. You may
get kicked yourself, or get smashed up
against the wall. The most effective thing to
do in most cases is to make a sudden, loud
noise, such as a shout, to distract the horses
from what they are doing, and to frighten
them out into the open. If this doesn't work,
I suspect that as a last resort, the old trick of
throwing a bucket of water on them would
do the trick. A well modulated yell has
always done the trick for me.

What if your horse backs *you* into a
corner? If this happens, and you think the
horse may kick, don't panic and try to run
out. Start talking, softly, cajolingly, and
don't stop. Watch the horse's ears and tail. If
he has backed up on you on purpose, his
ears will be back, his eyes warning. If his
ears aren't back, and if his haunch muscles
are relaxed, you may be able to put your
hand gently on his quarters, talking all the
while, and walk by, as he never meant to
corner you at all.

If his ears are back, he is warning you,
and you must be careful. Watch his tail and
hindquarters. His signal that he is about to
kick will usually be a clamping down of the

tail. Don't try to put your hand on him. Just talk and edge toward the door slowly. If he is very close to you take heart in the fact that if he does kick he will only get you with his hock. If you stay cool, and don't make any fast moves, even a horse that means business will usually let you out of the stall, not realizing you are moving for the door. A horse doesn't back you up against the wall just to be mean, he is afraid of you. He will be relieved when you get out; in fact, that is what he wants in the first place.

If you have a horse that habitually pins you against the wall when you go in the stall, or that is hard to catch in the stall, you will want to try to break him of this.

Horses that are hard to catch in the stall will usually do one of two things. They will either charge at you with teeth bared, trying to scare you away, and then whirl and at least pretend to try to kick at you, or they will dodge and whirl away when you approach, keeping their hindquarters toward you all the time. Both problems are tiresome, time-consuming, frightening, and at least potentially dangerous.

The horse that charges may sometimes be the easiest to cure. Generally a well-aimed swat on the nose, or even just a startling yell, will stop the horse once he has begun to run at you. Often the horse will have gotten into the habit of charging at you over the door of the stall as you walk by, not even waiting until you try to go in with him. Or he may charge at you when you go in to put his feed in the box or bucket. When he charges at you over the door, stand your ground, being prepared to punish him if he actually tries to bite you. This kind of horse has either gotten into the habit of being able to intimidate people into staying away from him, or he is so afraid of people that he feels he has to attack you before you attack him. In either case, you have to teach him 1) you are not afraid of him (even if you really are, you've got to convince *him* that you're not); 2) you won't hurt him unless he hurts you first; and 3) nothing bad will happen when he does let you catch him.

The first one of these things is probably the most important, from your standpoint anyway. The horse must learn that he cannot scare you away. Depending on how brave you are, and what kind of horse you are dealing with, you can do one of several things. If you are sure your horse is bluffing and is actually more afraid of you than you are of him, you may want to just stand your ground and call his bluff. Sooner or later he will learn that you will not back away, and he will give up charging at you. Some persistent horses may continue a token charge for years, never intending, or even really trying, to get you at all. We have an old mare that would charge everyone, even her owner, every time you went to catch her, and she never hurt anyone. Even now, after nearly ten years of retirement, she lays her ears back and threatens when you go up to her. It's just her habit. If your horse is a bluffer, you may be brave enough just to go ahead and catch him anyway, as we did with Shadow. But be careful and watch him, for someday he might mean business, or even just misjudge and get you by mistake.

If you have a horse that does mean business when he charges, you will have to take action. This kind of horse must learn that it hurts to bite, kick, or charge at people. He must learn to follow the rules. With the horse in the stall and the door closed, walk by. Carry a strap, short stick, or bat. If the horse rushes at you, raise the stick and slap him on the nose, just hard enough to scare him, and yell "NO!" or something loud, all at the same time, and keep on walking. The next time you go by, you may only have to raise your hand or warn with your voice, and eventually he will quit altogether, or at least learn to keep his distance. Don't threaten him until he threatens you, and if he doesn't come at you, call out his name and something nice as you go by to reward him for his good behavior.

After your horse accepts you at the door, try going in. At first, take a handful of grain and put it in the feed box when you open the door, if the box or bucket is by the door. When the horse comes up to take the feed, stand at the door, inside, talking to him quietly. If he threatens, threaten back, using your stick if necessary. Retreat only if you have to, for instance, if he whirls to kick. Sometimes a horse will charge only when you are feeding him, because he is defending his food. In that case it is necessary to teach the horse to stand back away from the box until you put the feed in and are out of the way. It is important to realize that some horses have what amounts to an obsession about this, and you should never bother this type of horse when he is eating, as it only makes him worse. But he must be taught not to interfere with you while you are placing the feed in the box. Don't be tempted to race in and out as fast as you can to stay out of his way, because this, too, will make him worse.

If you feel you need it, keep carrying your stick, and keep working at it until you can walk in and the horse greets you in a friendly manner, or at least doesn't attack. When you catch him, tie him to work on him in the stall until he accepts you and stops putting his ears back and threatening at all. Spend some time grooming him and being nice to him, so he learns to trust you. When he does not react unfavorably to you, you can leave him loose while you are in the stall, but keep an eye on him, and always stay between him and the door. As long as he puts his ears back at you when you approach, do not trust him in the stall untied, as he may try to back you in a corner.

The other kind of problem in the stall is the horse that retreats to a corner of the stall with his quarters aimed at you and refuses to let you get to his head. Unfortunately, this kind usually doesn't respond to grain, either.

We had a horse with this bad habit, and he was very hard to catch in the field, too. He just wouldn't let you get hold of his head or halter at all. If you went in his stall, he'd spin around and around, and finally pin you against the wall with his rear end. He never actually kicked anyone, but no one could catch him, either. He'd hold you against the wall until you gave up and went for the door.

We tried all kinds of sneaky ways of catching him, starting with using grain, and ending up using three or four people in the stall, but that just got him so shook up that we were afraid that he really would kick. It got so the only way to catch him was to open the door and try to catch him on his way out, which was definitely not the best way.

Finally one day I got tired of messing with him (he was a good teaching horse, once you caught him) that I took the long reins on the Western bridle and started swatting him on the hindquarters, keeping far enough away that if he kicked he couldn't get me. I whipped him with the ends of the reins until he finally turned around to face me, with his rear in the corner. Then I went in with him, and when he tried to whirl I hit him again. All this time I was shouting "Turn Around!" in time to my slaps with the reins. At last he was so scared of me that he just stood still when I went up to his head. Of course when I caught him I gave him a handful of grain and was quiet and gentle with him. Pretty soon he would turn around when you just tapped him on the rump and gave the command, and eventually he would face you with just the voice command. Of course, we always rewarded him with grain and gentle handling when he was good, and we went out of our way to catch him just to pet him, so he doesn't always associate being caught with work.

This approach worked with this horse, who was fairly aggressive naturally and is not particularly high strung. However, if your horse is the kind that is naturally jumpy, or that is really afraid of people in general, you will probably want to go through a more gentle approach of talking and waiting until the horse relaxes and turns around and accepts you. Some horses just cannot be bullied into behaving, some will only respond to kindness, and some may never get over their distrust of people entirely. Whichever way you choose, be careful, and try to be as patient as possible. If all your efforts seem to only make the situation worse, your only solution may be to sell the horse and try again.

Another problem in the stable is the cast

horse. This doesn't happen very often, but when it does it can be frightening, particularly if you are small like me. A horse is said to be cast when he gets down and is in such a position that he cannot get up again. Sometimes a horse will lie down in his stall and roll over so close to the wall that he can't get his legs under him to get up again, and he is so close that he can't roll back over. Or he may get his legs caught under the manger or under the side boards in the stall. A horse can even get his legs caught under the fence if he rolls over next to it.

When a horse is cast, you have to try to keep him calm, and try to roll him over or somehow get him into a position from which he can get up. It may be possible to remove part of the manger to release him. To keep the horse from struggling, hold his head down by placing your knee on his cheek bone and your hand on his nose above the nostrils and push down. You may need to put all or most of your weight on him if you are small, like me. To roll the horse over, you can put ropes around his front and hind legs, but if you do, make sure you have tied quick-release knots, because he will get up fast once he is in the right position.

If you have someone to help you, have them grasp the hind legs at the fetlock joints, and pull the feet of the horse as close to his belly as possible. Then you take his front legs and bend the feet back toward the elbows of the horse. This will cut down on the horse's ability to strike out in his efforts to rise, and will make it easier for you to roll him. Release his head before you try to move him, so you don't injure his neck. When you roll him over, get out of the way as fast as you can to let him get up.

If the horse is very large, or if he is very distressed and you are afraid he may injure himself, you may want to tranquilize him and use ropes and pulleys to get him over. A call to the vet is in order for this, and if you can't reach a vet, your blacksmith has undoubtedly had experience in using ropes and pulleys on horses.

If you have to pull the horse out from under something, do not pull him by the legs. Have one or two people grasp him by the tail as close to his body as they can get, and pull. We did this to a horse that had fallen in a horse trailer once, and it worked beautifully. Once the horse is up, get rid of whatever it was he got caught under, or fix it so it cannot happen again.

When the horse is up, walk him around a bit to check for drastic injuries, and to calm him down. Keep an eye on him for a few hours, and don't feed or water him right away. Give him time to calm down internally, and keep an eye on him for a few days in case he has pulled some muscles or otherwise injured himself.

Another problem that occurs in the stable is the horse that is hard to tie. Some horses won't tie because they have broken a halter or rope and know they can get away. Others may have been frightened while tied, or hurt, and they won't tie because they are afraid to be confined. Some may get this way because they have been tied up and left for long periods of time.

Never tie a horse and go off and leave him for more than a few minutes. If you have to go away, put him in a stall, a paddock, or (if you're at a horse show) put him in the trailer or van. Your horse should not be expected to stand tied for more than a half an hour or so.

If your horse is a halter breaker, you can run an unbreakable rope around the horse's neck, tie it in a non-slip knot (like a bowline), and run it down through the noseband of the halter. The halter will keep the rope

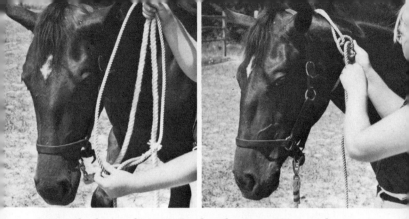

Tying the horse that tries to break away: First, make a lasso loop and put it around horse's neck. Then tie a knot so the rope is no longer in a slip knot.

Bring rope down through halter so it cannot slip down neck, and tie it with about 2½ feet of slack at the level of the horse's withers.

from dropping down too low, but will not take any of the strain if the horse pulls back. Once the horse is securely tied to something that he cannot break or pull down (like a tree, for instance) walk away and leave him. Keep an eye on him from a distance where he cannot see you, and let him stand for a few minutes. If he stands without argument, turn him loose in a few minutes. If he fights, let him fight until he gets tired and lets up. Then turn him loose as soon as he stops fighting, to show that something good happens when he stands still. Do this several times a day until he doesn't fight at all.

With the horse that fights because he is afraid that something will hurt him, things may take a little longer. The procedure is basically the same, except that instead of walking off and leaving him, you stay with the horse and pet him, talk to him, groom him. Get him to realize that you will not hurt him, and that being tied up will not hurt him. Always turn him loose while he is calm and relaxed, not when he is trying to get loose. Do not get worried if he sits back and leans on the rope, as long as he does not get it wrapped around his nose. As long as he is not choking, and does not have a foot over the rope, he isn't going to hurt himself.

Never get mad and tie the horse with unbreakable rope and go off and leave him. He could panic and fight until he kills himself. If he throws himself and can't get up, or if he is choking, cut the rope or untie the knot, if possible.

The most common habitual vices in the stable are probably cribbing and weaving. A horse is said to be a cribber when he habitually sets his front teeth on the edge of the fence or manger and sucks in air, usually making a grunting sound in the process. This "vice," which is usually considered an unsoundness, amounts to an addiction of the horse to swallowing air. It wears down the front edges of the upper incisors, causes disturbances in the digestive tract, as well as being dangerous to the horse's health because of the danger of swallowing splinters and dirt. A cribber will practice his vice on anything hard enough to set his teeth into, and if he can't find anything to grab, he may pick up windsucking, which is cribbing without biting onto anything.

Cribbing usually begins because of boredom combined with a very nervous temperament, and sometimes because of hunger and boredom combined, when a horse is confined to a stall for long periods of time. It is not infrequent among race horses. Horses can also pick up the habit by watching other horses do it. Once the habit is confirmed, there seems to be no real cure. Painting all horizontal surfaces the horse can reach with specially made substances (such as Chew-Stop) may help for a while, but a confirmed cribber will ignore the bad taste and smell and go to work anyway.

Cribbing straps may cut down on the amount of air taken in, and some of them act on the principle that when the horse swallows the strap causes pain. (The strap doesn't interfere with normal eating because it only works when the horse's head is up, and he can't crib with his head down.) Unfortunately, however, a true cribber would rather crib and hurt than give it up. There are specially made muzzles that are supposed to prevent the horse from setting his teeth on anything, but a smart horse can learn to use the muzzle to crib on, in which case it is a help to him, rather than a hindrance. I have personally never seen a cure for a cribber. The best solution is to keep one out of the stable as much as possible. Keep him busy, pasture him with other horses, and when you do have to stable him, keep him away from the other horses if possible, so they don't pick it up.

A weaver is a horse that has gotten into the habit of rocking from side to side on his front feet in his stall. Like cribbing, this is a nervous habit apparently caused by having nothing to do for long periods of time. A weaver will stand at his stall door, rocking back and forth, until he must surely be dizzy, and is probably lulled much as a baby is by rocking. He will wear holes in the floor under his front feet, and may even develop foot and leg problems in the process. There are no real cures for weavers, except for keeping them out of the stable, although I did see a trick that worked on at least one horse with this problem. The owner tied a bunch of tin cans on ropes hanging from the ceiling of the stall so they rattled together when the horse walked around, and the noise was either so aggravating or so interesting that the horse forgot all about weaving and spent his time playing with his new toy. I have also heard of rubber tires being used.

Both cribbers and weavers are best kept out of the stable and on a regular riding or exercise schedule. Cribbers and weavers are almost always hard keepers, perhaps because of their nervous temperaments, and perhaps just because of the extra energy they burn indulging in their neuroses.

The last stable problem to discuss is simply fussing—fussing when the horse is being shod, or being clipped, or being doctored. If the horse has been trained to stand and lead as I have recommended, and has not gotten into the habit of pushing his handler around, this will not often be a problem. Sometimes any horse can be a problem, however, especially if he is hurt or particularly thin skinned. Occasionally simply distracting him by jangling the lead shank will be enough, and sometimes putting one hand on his nose and holding his ear with the other will help. The commonest remedy, however, is to apply a twitch.

A twitch is a wooden handle some eighteen inches to two feet in length with a cord or rope loop, six inches in diameter, running through a hole in one end of it. Most often twitches are improvised by drilling a hole in a sawed-off broom handle and making a loop out of clothes line, but fancy ones can also be purchased. The twitch is applied to the horse's nose to cause enough pain to distract him from whatever is being done to him, though the key word is distract, rather than pain.

To apply a twitch, simply put your left hand through the loop and grasp the horse's nose with it. Adjust the rope past the end of the upper lip, and twist the handle with your right hand until it is firmly in place. The amount of pressure you need to apply will never be very great, but you will be surprised how easily you will be able to do things that would otherwise be difficult or impossible. After the twitch has been removed, the horse's nose should be rubbed to restore circulation. If you have any question about using a twitch, ask your vet or blacksmith to show you how.

Part II

HEALTH CARE

7

Hoof Care

GOOD HOOF CARE is a team effort between the horse's owner and the farrier (blacksmith). The owner, unless he is a farrier too, cannot do the job alone, and even the best efforts by a blacksmith can be wasted by a careless owner. The owner and the blacksmith have to work together, calling in the vet occasionally for extreme problems.

First of all, find a good blacksmith in your area. Look for someone who has had some years of experience, preferably, and who has a good reputation. Sometimes a few questions at a track or racing stable can turn up a good one for you. Racing smiths have to be good to keep their jobs. If a track farrier is too busy to do outside work, he may be able to recommend someone else to you. Sometimes a graduate of a qualified farrier's school can be good, provided it is indeed a good school, and that he was indeed a good student. Never let a friend "practice" on your horse's feet! Horseshoeing is an art that takes years of careful study and experience to perfect.

If you can tell a good shoeing job when you see one, a good way of finding a blacksmith may be to go to shows and observe the kind of work done on the horses there, and then ask who does the jobs you admire. Or you could ask your vet to recommend someone. If you have trouble finding someone with a good reputation, remember that with the exception of a real amateur, any blacksmith is better than none.

When you call a blacksmith, make up your mind before you start to allow him to handle your horse as he sees fit. Do not interfere unless you *know* he is doing harm to the horse—it is probable that he has had more experience with horses than you have.

It is usual for a horse to need a blacksmith every five or six weeks, although variations do occur. Some horses have naturally hard, tough feet, and if they are kept barefoot and ridden regularly their feet may wear down by themselves and not need trimming as often. If, however, the horse's feet don't get long because they split and break off, he does need a blacksmith. Horses with brittle feet may need to be shod, or may need extra care when barefoot to keep their feet from breaking off.

Then, too, some horses may need their feet trimmed and shaped, and reshod, every four weeks or so. A horse that has been foundered (see chapter on Illnesses), a horse that has shallow or contracted heels, one that is prone to splits and cracks in the hooves, or that is prone to thrush (a fungus affecting the frog of the hoof) and has it more or less chronically, will need extra care by both owner and blacksmith. With time and good care, all of these problems can be helped, if not cured. But without the extra care, they may deteriorate, and the horse will surely suffer.

Horses with bad feet may have to be kept out of the stall as much as possible. Problems that are aggravated by damp conditions, such as thrush or founder, may be helped by keeping the horse at pasture, provided that the field is grassy, not rocky and hard. On the other hand, problems such as dry feet, split or cracked hooves that are very brittle, may be aggravated by staying on hard, dry ground.

Even though some horses have naturally

good feet and others have feet more prone to problems, none of the problems would occur if the care they received was adequate. Some occur from problems in feeding: a young horse's feet can be irreparably damaged by poor nutrition, and founder is often a result of errors in judgment in feeding and watering. Thrush is often caused by keeping the horse in too damp surroundings and not cleaning the feet often enough. Dry, brittle feet may be a result of a poor diet combined with a lack of hoof dressing when the feet get extra dry. Other problems may arise because, while food and water are given properly and the stable may be kept well, the horse is ridden too hard on hard surfaces, or is improperly shod, or not shod when he should be, or not trimmed and shod often enough.

You should check, and clean out, all four feet on each horse daily. Smell each foot, and if it smells bad, assume the horse has or is getting thrush, and douse the foot with either a prepared thrush remedy, or Chlorox. If the frog is black and peeling, or oozing a nasty discharge the thrush is bad and you will know it by the strong odor. Douse the hoof daily, and when the blacksmith comes again, draw it to his attention.

Picking up the front feet: 1. Stand at the horse's shoulder, facing his hindquarters. 2. Run your hand down his leg to just above the fetlock.

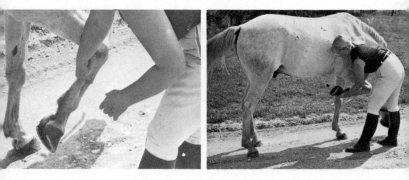

3. Push the horse with your shoulder to shift his weight to the opposite foot, and pull up on the fetlock. 4. Then bring the foot up to a comfortable height to examine it or pick it out.

To work on a foot, bring it under your leg and hold it by squeezing your knees together. When you decide to put the foot down, don't drop it; lower it slowly with your hand on the cannon bone.

He will test the hoof to see if any soreness is there, and he can find any deeply imbedded thrush you may have missed. He can also put medicine (usually iodine) down into the cleft of the frog, or cut away part of it if necessary. Do not poke around too much yourself if you do not know where to look, and do not use anything sharp. Your blacksmith may slice off a lot of the frog to get to the seat of the problem, but he knows how to do it, and you don't.

If your horse has the tell-tale rings and dished feet that mean he has been foundered, pay special attention to his feet. He will be more prone to foot problems than the average horse, and founder can reoccur. If you have a very small pony, or one of those large horses with tiny feet, take extra good care of them, too, as they are more prone to founder than other horses, due to the added burden of their weight on very small feet.

If your horse's feet seem dry, put hoof dressing on them. Paint it on the heel and around the coronary band. Commercial hoof dressings can be used, or you can make a mixture of pine tar and neatsfoot oil. If your horse's feet have thrush and seem soft, do not use hoof dressing unless recommended by your blacksmith or vet.

If you have your horse shod, the problem of missing or loose shoes will undoubtedly arise. Sometimes it is impossible to get the blacksmith when you want him, as I'm sure you know. If your horse gets a loose shoe, don't ride him until it is taken care of. A loose shoe may throw him off balance, come off or break and cut him. It may even slide over to one side and cut his opposite fetlock. If he loses a shoe, or one gets loose, call the blacksmith and tell him it is a dire emergency. (Otherwise he may not come right away.)

If the horse loses a shoe, and if the hoof is broken off badly, or if you know that his feet break easily, do not ride him. If he has good, hard feet you might ride him lightly, on soft ground, keeping an eye on his feet. You don't want to wear the hoof down shorter than it should be to be shod.

If your horse gets a shoe loose, and it slides around so you are worried that it might cut him, there are two things you can do. If you can get the blacksmith the same day, you could put him in a stall and wait. Or you may want to get someone else to take the shoe off for you. Get someone you know, and trust, and have him gently work the shoe off. If you have ever watched your

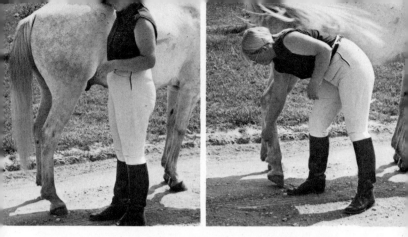

To pick up a rear foot: 1. Stand at the horse's stifle, facing the rear, hand on croup. 2. Run your hand down the leg to just above the fetlock. Pull and lean on the horse so he tips the foot up.

3. Bring your hand down to the pastern and pull the leg up, using your other hand to push the horse over. Try not to pull the leg sideways. 4. To hold the leg up, hook your elbow over the hock and bring your knee up to support the leg. This frees your hands.

blacksmith at work, and you should watch him, you will know how it is done, and you can either do it yourself or supervise whoever does do it. Do not try to rasp the edges off, as they will tend to wear off by themselves, and you might take too much off.

If your horse should somehow get a shoe caught on the fence or something, do not panic. If it is anything at all movable or breakable, try to dismantle it or cut it off the main object. Give the horse some feed to keep him distracted, and gently work it off the shoe, or work the shoe off the hoof. Tie the horse short to keep him from walking off, if he ties well and calmly. If you cannot get it off, call the vet first, because he can tranquilize the horse if necessary. If you cannot reach the vet, then call the blacksmith.

8

Grooming

GROOMING FOR HORSES, as for people, is a matter of hygiene. Grooming helps keep the horse healthy by stimulating the skin, keeping the pores clear, stimulating hair growth and helping the distribution of natural oils. It also makes the horse look and smell better, and keeps you cleaner.

Full-scale grooming does not have to be done daily, particularly if the horse is kept on pasture, as he will stay fairly clean naturally. In addition, when a horse is kept out, the dandruff and oils that build up on his skin help to protect him from the heat (or cold), and the flies. The legs, however, should be cleaned more often, especially before riding, to prevent sores and cracks developing from dirt encrusted on the pasterns and heels. And of course, the head, back and girth area must be groomed before riding, paying special attention to the places where the girth goes.

I personally do not believe in using a metal curry comb on a horse at all, except on very heavy coats. Metal curry combs are useful for cleaning brushes, but they can damage the horse's skin if used improperly. To get the point, just run a metal curry over the skin of your arm, lightly, and then remember that a horse's skin is so sensitive that he can feel a fly land on him.

Use a rubber curry comb vigorously in swirling motions to remove caked dirt and mud, and loose hair and dandruff. Use it more gently on the face and legs. Make sure that you get between the front legs and on the stomach, gently.

Use the dandy brush (hard bristles) vigorously all over, going with the lay of the hair. Go gently around the face and under the stomach and between the fore legs. This brings the dirt up to the surface, and stimulates the skin.

Use the body brush (soft bristles) to pick up the dirt brought up by the dandy brush and to put a gleam to the coat. Use it around the eyes and ears, and under the jaw. Then use the curry comb to clean the brush.

If the horse flinches from whatever brush

you are using, go more lightly or use a softer brush. He may also flinch from bruises you are otherwise unaware of. Pay close attention to his back if he flinches while you are working there; feel for soft lumps or heat.

Comb out or brush the mane and tail often enough to keep the tangles down or you may end up having to cut out large pieces of hair to get out mats and burrs.

If your horse has a lot of hair on his fet-

Clipping the fetlocks with electric clippers: 1. Holding the foot with one hand, use the clippers against the grain of the hair, bringing them up over the coronary band and fetlock. 2. Still working upwards, clip the hair from the fetlock and the back of the pastern.

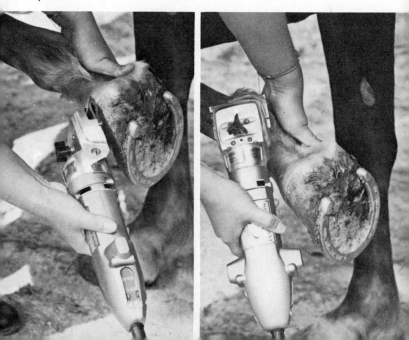

3. Moving the hand back to hold the leg just above the fetlock, clip the inside of the pastern and fetlock.
4. Now bring the leg forward and rest the hoof on your knee. Clip upwards from the coronet, blending the hair in over the fetlock.

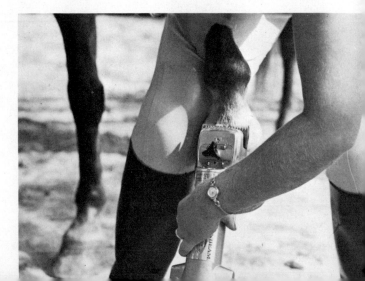

5. *Trimming the hind feet is a little harder. Follow the same procedure, except for the hair on the end of the fetlock, which is easier done with the foot on the ground. 6. Compare the hind legs for neatness. (The horse needs shoeing.)*

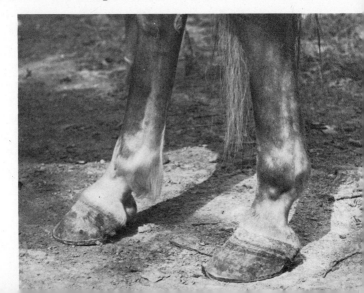

locks, it may be easier to keep his legs clean if you cut it. It will also improve his looks. Of course electric clippers do the job best, and if you use them be careful to keep the head flat against the hair to keep from gouging or burning. While large animal clippers work much better and do the job faster, small animal clippers will work on fetlocks and other small jobs. You may find that small clippers will not cut against the hair, and you may have to use it with the lay of the hair. Large clippers work best on the fetlocks when you bring them up from the hoof over the coronary band, and then taper off above the fetlock. Then bring it down from just behind the knee to blend into the clipped portion.

If you use hand clippers, be careful not to pinch the ergots (callous-like bumps on the fetlock joint). If you use scissors, cut up or down, instead of sideways, to make it look smoother and to avoid cutting chunks of hair out.

While it may seem at first to be warmer to leave the long hair on the fetlocks in winter, remember that the horse's lower legs are often wet in winter and the dirt and mud in the hair may turn to ice. In cold weather, cut the hair on the legs so it is approxi-

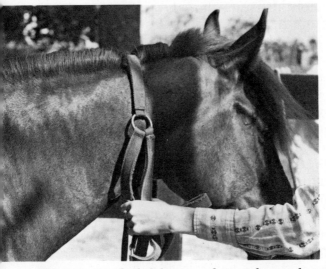

The mane can be left long on pleasure horses, but the hair sticking up where the bridle path has grown out looks ragged.

If you want to trim the bridle path, loop the halter around the horse's neck so he cannot move away, but you can work behind his ears. Clip from the sides over the mane, then up and back along the mane bed.

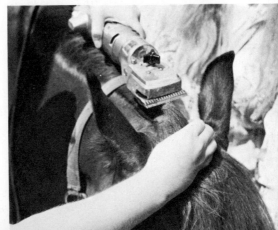

mately the same length as the hair on the rest of the body.

If your horse has a thick mane, it will probably be handy to cut a "bridle path" behind the ears. This path can be a few inches wide, to make the bridle or halter crownpiece fit more neatly, or it can extend farther down the neck, whichever looks best to you. If you do cut a bridle path, point the clippers or scissors away from the ears (towards the withers), in case the horse throws his head up unexpectedly.

Most of the other grooming you will do on your horse will be in preparation for a show. You should always remember that the better you and your horse look, the more chance you will have of winning a ribbon, and that goes for any kind of horse show or trail ride where the judging is up to the opinion of the judge, rather than on time or faults. Bringing a horse to a show or ride out of shape and ill-groomed will practically eliminate all possibility of the judge admiring you and your horse to the point of wanting to pin you in a class.

First of all, your horse should be in peak condition before you consider showing. A horse that is either underweight or too fat, that is unthrifty, or that is in poor muscular condition, should not be expected to perform well enough to win ribbons. It will only embarrass you and possibly injure the horse to show him in such condition. Your horse should be sleek, well rounded and vibrantly healthy. If he is, whatever conformation faults he may have will be minimized.

Some horses seem to keep a real bloom to their coats naturally, but others may need special attention to bring out the shine. Special coat conditioners added to the feed are often an aid. Your feed store may stock some of these supplements and your saddlery shop undoubtedly will; you can ask your vet to recommend one for you. Start giving any supplement several months before you expect to show. Don't expect them to work overnight.

Regular grooming is an aid to a soft, smooth coat. Pay particular attention to the use of the dandy brush, as it stimulates natural oils which give the coat that shine. Again, start ahead of time, giving the horse at least a month to get in shape.

A horse with a dark coat may benefit from wearing a lightweight sheet out in the field to keep the sun from bleaching the coat. However, stabling the horse during the day and turning him out at night accomplishes the same thing.

Have the horse shod a week to two weeks in advance of a show. Give him the few days before the show in case the nails were set too close and he is a little tender.

Even if you show only in halter (or conformation) classes, it is important to have the horse in good muscular condition. At halter the judge wants to see a well-conditioned, fit horse, and a performance horse will need to be in good shape to hold up to a day's showing. He cannot be expected to compete if he is soft and flabby. If the horse is too young to be ridden you can longe him or pony him (lead from another horse) to get him fit.

In addition, you will want to get the horse schooled to get him performing as well as possible. This goes for performance at halter as well as under saddle. Take him to a show only when he is performing the required movements well at home. Don't expect him to learn it in the show ring.

All right, you say, but what about grooming? Well, these first things I have discussed are grooming, just as brushing, clipping and braiding are. Conditioning the horse is as much a part of horse grooming as exercising is a part of grooming for people.

Now that the horse is fit, shod, and well-schooled, what about his appearance? Take a good look at your horse. If you are showing English, you will want to groom him according to what division you will show in. If you are showing in a particular breed class, you will want to find a book on this breed and read up on the requirements for showing. If you show in pleasure classes, you will want to leave the mane and tail free. If you show Saddle Seat, Arabians and Morgans show with manes and tails long and free, Three-Gaited Saddlebreds show with mane roached while Five-Gaited Saddlebreds show with long mane and tail. Tennessee Walking Horses show with long mane and tail. If you show in hunter classes, the mane and tail are braided.

If you are going to show with the horse's mane long, you will want to thin it if it is particularly thick, so that it lies close to the neck. If you braid, you will need to thin and shorten the mane to about 3 to 4 inches long and quite thin. To pull a horse's mane, comb it thoroughly to the right side of the horse's neck. There are several ways you can pull a mane. One is to wear gloves, and pull a few of the longer hairs out at a time, working from the poll downward, until the mane is the right length and thickness. Don't try this without well-fitting gloves, or your fingers will be so sore you can't ride!

Another method is to use a "pulling comb," which is a mane comb with shorter, sharper teeth. To use the pulling comb, separate 2 or 3 inches of mane, back-comb it until there are only 8 or 10 hairs left in the comb, twist the comb around these hairs, and yank them out. Repeat as necessary, combing the mane smooth between pulls. This method is faster, but the horse may object if he is sensitive about this. Whoever said that horses didn't have any feelings in their mane obviously never tried to pull one. It may help to work up and down the neck to keep the horse from getting sore in any one spot. If the mane is long and thick, plan to take two or three days to finish it.

There is really no substitute for pulling a mane, to get it looking really natural, but if you just don't have the time to do it, or if the horse really objects to having it pulled, you may want to try an alternative method. You will need a pair of thinning scissors and either a hair razor or a mat-splitter, which is a razor used on long-coated dogs to remove mats and tangles. Both of these items can be gotten at a dog grooming salon or a kennel. They cost about $2.50 each. After combing the mane out carefully, thin it by using the scissors up and down the mane, until it is braiding thickness. Test it by braiding several braids to see if it will make very flat braids. Wearing gloves, give the horse a razor cut, using the razor at various lengths on the hair to give it a naturally uneven appearance. The gloves are to protect you in case the horse moves; the mat-splitter is designed so it will not cut the animal. Don't forget to thin the forelock too.

After you have thinned and/or shortened the mane, cut a bridle patch behind the horse's ears, either with scissors or clippers. If you use scissors, cut lengthwise along the neck for a smoother appearance. Many people like to leave a longer bridle path on horses that wear the mane long, particularly if the horse's neck is a little thick.

Next comes braiding the mane, a tedious job for which there is no known substitute. However, it can be considerably less tiresome if you plan it right. Get something comfortable to stand on that won't tip over easily. Even if you can reach the horse's poll easily, unless you stand on something, you will have to keep your arms at an

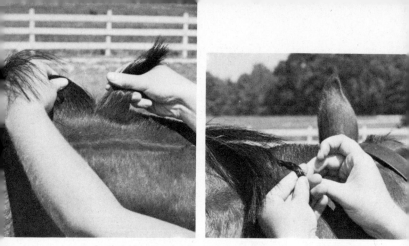

To braid the mane, first separate one or two inches of hair to make a braid. (The thinner the mane, the more hair you can use.) 2. Braid the three strands down to the end.

Tie the end of the braid together tightly and fold it under, fitting the ends tightly against the mane. Then sew the braid together, bringing the needle up from the bottom and winding it around the whole braid. Continue down the neck the same way.

uncomfortably high position for fairly long periods of time. Pick a cool, shady spot to work in, or in the barn, if the lighting is good enough. Put fly repellent on the horse to cut down on his moving around. (Put it on yourself, too, as you will need both hands.) Tie the horse short so he can't move around too much. Don't wear gloves, as you will need your fingers unimpeded. Plan to braid no earlier than the night before the show, or the horse will probably rub some braids out. Assemble your tools — scissors, large needle with a big eye, heavy duty thread of a color as close to the color of the mane as possible, or at least darker than the mane, and a mane comb. Wear a smock or shirt with large pockets to put your gear in. If you have long hair, tie it or pin it back so it doesn't get in your face.

You may want to wet the mane to make it

To braid the forelock, make a single braid and sew it as on the neck. You may have to thin it first to get it to look neat.

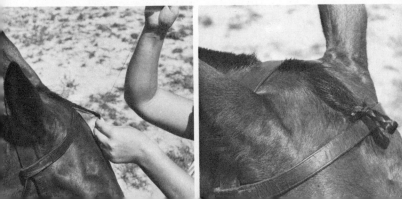

lie flatter, though this tends to make it slippery. Thread the needle with a piece of
thread that will be 12 to 18 inches long
when doubled and tie a big knot. Slip the
needle into your shirt or pants leg in a place
where you can reach it without looking, if
possible. I don't advise holding it in your
teeth, if for no other reason than you will
probably drop it when you yell at the horse
for moving.

Starting at the poll, with the mane
combed to the right side of the neck (to be
out of the way when mounting), separate an
inch or two of mane, depending on how
thick the hair. You can put more hair into a
braid on a horse with very fine hair than one
with thicker hair. Braid the hair very tightly
down as far as you can.

Holding the end of the braid tightly in
one hand, take the needle and thread it
through the end of the crossed pieces of
hair as close to the end as will hold the
braid together. Put the needle in from the
bottom, and loop it around and through
until the end of the braid is secured.

Next, double the braid under and wedge
the end up under the top of the braid snugly
against the hair bed of the mane, making
the braid lie as flat as possible. Bring the
needle up through the bottom and sew the

braid to itself at the hair bed as tightly and as snugly as you can. Knot the thread under the braid and cut close to the knot. (I find manicure scissors handy for this.) The braid should be small and flat.

Continue down the horse's neck, being careful to get all the hairs, until you reach the withers. You may want to leave the last few hairs loose at the withers. Then braid the forelock in one braid. You may have to pull the forelock to get it to make a neat braid.

A few don'ts: Don't scissor off all those little hairs sticking up around the braids as they will grow out looking even worse, and as hairs break off you will cut more and more until the horse has no mane at all. Don't use yarn, or colored rubber bands, or brightly colored or contrasting thread. It looks very amateurish. If you must use rubber bands instead of thread, use plain ones. (Rubber bands are easier to put in than thread, but they also fall out easily! And they look terrible.)

You may want to take a pair of small scissors to the show to cut the thread out after the show. Don't leave the braids in more than one night after the show or the horse will rub his mane out.

Braiding the tail will require a bit more

skill, but once the technique is mastered, you will find it surprisingly easy.

If your horse is touchy about having his hindquarters handled, you may want to spend some time handling him and combing his tail to get him to stand still. If he is the kind of horse that does not object to being handled when he is eating, you may want to do his tail while he is being fed.

If the horse's tail is extremely long and/or thick, you will want to thin and shorten it. This can be done by pulling or by cutting. You may want to "bang" the tail by cutting it straight across, just below the hocks. This looks attactive on a big hunter or show jumper. Otherwise you will want to shorten the tail and thin it to look natural and to enhance the horse's appearance. Shaping the tail is always done in reference to the horse's size and build. Stand back and look at your horse from the back and the side. Remembering that narrowing and thinning the tail tends to make the hindquarters look larger, decide whether or not you will want to make the top of the tail thinner, and how much you should shorten the tail. Western horses usually wear the tail at or slightly above the hocks, English hunters to the

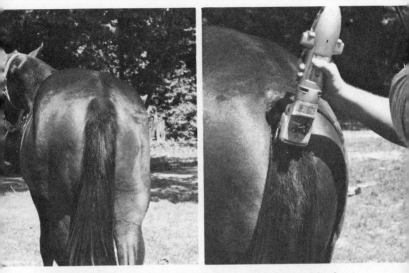

The tail before clipping. This filly rubbed has rubbed the short hairs at the top until they are frizzy. The clipping is done downwards, pulling the tail up to get all the side hairs.

hock or slightly below, and some of the breeds with an even longer tail. (Check the books on the particular breeds for specific information on this.)

Pulling the tail is usually easier and less time-consuming than doing the mane. Wearing gloves, simply separate the hair and pull out the longest hairs several at a time. Yank hard to pull the hair out cleanly; otherwise the horse may object to having

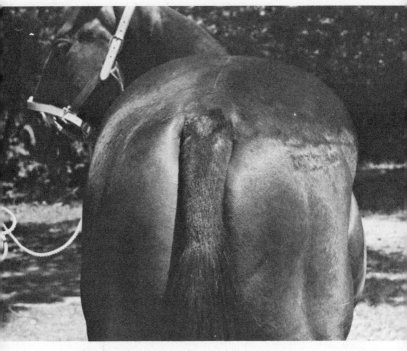

The finished job, clipped down to where a braided tail would end. Note how much wider the hindquarters appear.

what feels like to him his whole tail pulled out.

The alternative to pulling the tail is to cut the long pieces out with scissors, working on the inside layers of hair. Leave the long hairs on the upper half of the tail; pull the longest hairs from the lower half to thin and shorten. If you want the tail to be long and thin, pull the shorter hairs from the bottom half.

To braid the tail, first comb and smooth the hairs on the upper part of the tail as much as possible. With your needle threaded and secured in a handy place, stand directly behind the horse. You can start from either side but since I usually start from the left I will describe it that way. Working as close to the top of the tail as possible, take a small stand of hairs with your left hand, and then one on the right side across from it with your right. (See illustrations.) Twist these two strands around each other very tightly.

Braiding the tail. 1. Begin by taking a strand of hair from either side, as high as you can get, using the longer hairs. 2. Twist these two strands together to make one strand, which will be the center strand of your braid.

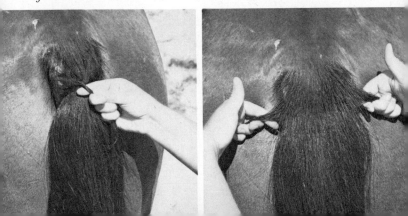

To braid the tail you will make a "French" braid, using one piece from each side and braiding into the ends of the pieces above. When you have the first two pieces of hair twisted together, they become the middle strand of the braid. Now pull a strand from the left side and braid it over the middle strand, then one from the right side and braid it over that. Keep repeating this, keeping it as tight as possible and using small, uniform strands, until you get about halfway down the tail, or until you have passed the curve of the buttocks. When you have gone as far down the tail as you wish to braid, braid the middle strand out to the end in a regular braid. Sew the end as you did the end of the braids on the mane, and then either turn it under and sew

3. Pull a strand from each side, alternating sides, and braid each into the center strand as tightly as you can. 4. Continue braiding strands into the center strand, left, right, left, etc. Keep it tight!

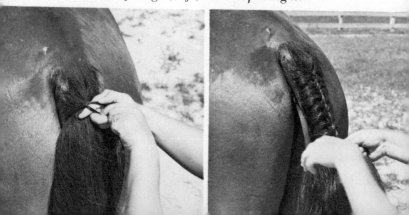

it into the bottom of the French braid, or roll it upwards in a tight coil and sew it into the tail at the end of the braid.

You will find it helpful to examine some braided tails at shows, and if possible, to get someone to show you how to do this. After some practice, however, it should become fairly easy for you. The hardest part of it is to get the braid tight enough, but again, practice makes perfect.

After the tail is braided, you may want to wrap it to keep the horse from rubbing it out. To bandage the tail, start at the top as high as you can reach, and wind the bandage snugly down to just below the braid, and then wind back up to the middle and pin it. Use a regular leg bandage, track bandage or Ace bandage. Dampen it first by

5. *Turn the end of the braid under, as with the mane, and sew it down, or roll the braid up tightly in a roll. Cover with a damp tail bandage to keep the horse from rubbing it down.*

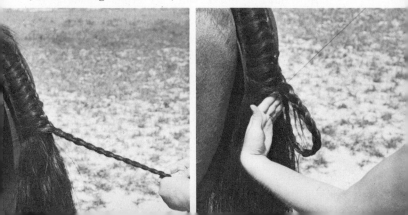

wetting it and wringing it out. This helps the hair to lie flat.

If you show Western, you will want to either shorten and thin the mane so that it lies well and is fairly short (hangs about halfway down the neck), or you can roach the mane, which means to clip it off entirely, except the forelock. You can roach the mane best with electric clippers, although a satisfactory job can be done with a pair of sharp scissors and strong hands. It is customary on Western horses to leave a wider bridle path, sometimes nearly halfway down the neck. A wider bridle path makes the throatlatch look more refined. It seldom makes a horse with a thin neck look

1. Before roaching, this filly's neck looks thicker than it really is. She is uneasy about clippers, so I start away from the head with a reassuring hand on her neck. Use the clippers up across the mane on each side, then finish by running up and down the neck. 2. Using clippers nearer the head after doing one side. Working near the head I run my variable speed clippers at the slower (and thus quieter) speeds. Note that the filly is now considerably more relaxed.

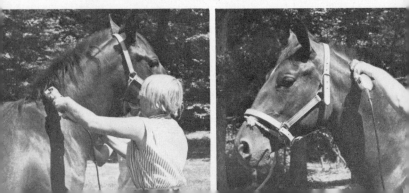

3. *By now she has completely accepted the noise and I can finish up behind the between the ears. You can see her relaxation, compared with the previous picture, by the fact that her nostrils aren't even flared. 4. The finished mane gives her a cleaner, trimmer appearance. Remember, though, that roaching the mane tends to make the head look bigger, so take an honest look at your horse before you start! It takes a little time to undo.*

good to roach the mane, but it may improve the appearance of a horse with a thick neck or a very bushy mane.

Once the horse's mane and tail are taken care of, you will want to trim the long hairs, if any, from around his jaw and chin, and remove the excess hair from around the fetlocks and pasterns as explained earlier. If you will show in halter classes, or if you

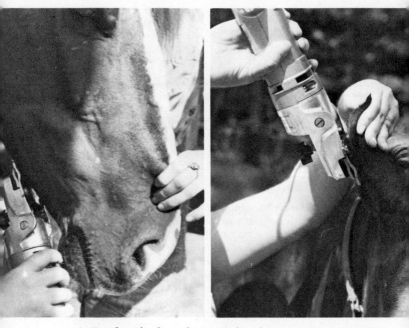

1. To clip the long hairs under the jaw, clip upwards to make the hair lie flat when finished. 2. You must clip against the hair inside the ears, so clip downwards, but be very careful not to cut the ear. Many horses object to this, and I would advise against it unless you can protect the horse from flies.

keep your horse stabled and protected from flies, you may also want to clip around the face and clip the insides of the ears. However, if the horse will be pastured, re-

member that the hair inside the ears helps
to protect him from flies. Small animal
clippers may be easier to use to clip inside
the ears.

If your horse is fit and in good health, he
need never be bathed at all. However, a
white or grey horse may have stains that
will not brush out, and a horse with a poor
coat may benefit from a bath. Always try to
bathe the horse several days before a show
to allow the natural oils to return; otherwise
the coat will be dull. Of course there are
sprays that will add a shine to the coat, but
there is no substitute for good health.

To give a bath, pick a warm day, not
windy, or keep the horse in a sheltered area
out of draft. You can bring him in from riding
a bit hot, if you like. Try to give the bath on
a grassy spot so he doesn't splash mud up
on his legs and belly when he moves
around. A hose is handy, but some horses
just refuse to stand still for one. If you don't
use a hose, use a bucket and a sponge, and
use the soap more sparingly.

If you use a hose, use a nozzle and adjust
it to a fine spray, rather than using a hard
stream of water. Do not use the hose on the
horse's head. Collect your tools first:
bucket, sponge, sweat scraper, rags, sham-

poo. (Use a specially made shampoo for horses, or a mild human shampoo. I use Johnson's Baby Shampoo with success, and one of the special brands for gray or silver hair for gray or white horses.) Wear old clothes and expect to get wet. Don't be tempted to go barefooted, as the horse will undoubtedly stamp around at a crucial moment. Use a nylon or rope halter so you don't ruin a leather one by getting it wet, and either get someone to hold the horse or tie him with something unbreakable. If your horse is unreliable about being tied, this is not the time to test him; have someone hold him. If someone holds him, it is wise to put a control halter on him as he is likely to jump around. (See pictures) However, do not put the chain or shank in a control position over the nose or under the chin, or tie a slip knot around the neck if you tie him.

If you use a hose, approach the horse with a dry hose first, to let him get accustomed to it. Place it on his back and run it down his sides a few times, until he is relaxed about it. If he is afraid of it dry, he will really react when water comes out of it.

When he has accepted the hose without water, take it a few feet away and turn the water on, letting him see it. Approach him again, with it down at your side, bringing it up slowly near his head so he can sniff at it if he wants. He may even want to drink from it. Using a slow, fine spray, gently splash it on his legs or over his back, going slowly. Give yourself plenty of time, and leave enough time before it cools off in the evening for the horse to dry.

Once you have wet the horse all over, whether with the hose or with a sponge, shampoo him thoroughly. This means all over his body, but not necessarily a lot of shampoo in any one place. If your horse tends to throw his head around, you may not want to soap his head at all. When he is soaped, use the dandy brush dipped in water to scrub him, brushing him just as you would if he were dry. Brush his mane thoroughly, and his tail. Use the sponge on his head and around his ears, and up under his belly. Pay particular attention to his knees, hocks, elbows, and the backs of the pasterns, as these are the areas most likely to have grass stains. When you have worked the soap in well, turn the fine spray on the hose again and soak the horse again thoroughly, or use a sponge. Then use the sweat scraper to get the water and soap out of the coat. Rinse him like this two or three times, or until you are sure all the shampoo is out. You may want to pour bucketfuls of water over his mane and tail, if he will stand for it. You can use bluing on a white horse with success, but don't use too much, or the horse will have a blue tint to his coat. It is particularly important to get all the shampoo out of the coat of a dark colored horse, as it will flake and look like dandruff.

After the horse's bath, first move him out of the wet area to dry grass or straw so he doesn't splash dirt and water up on his legs and belly. Then dry him with a sweat scraper and a big sponge. If you have some towels handy you can also rub him down with these to help dry him. Then you can either leave him tied in the shade, if the flies aren't bad, or put him in his stall until he dries. If the weather is at all cool, walk him dry, or if you put him in the stall, tie him up and put a lightweight sheet on him, to keep him from catching cold or rolling. After he is dry, brush him thoroughly with a clean brush to bring up the oil in his coat.

Because shampooing removes so much oil from the coat, you won't ordinarily want to give your horse a full-scale soap and water bath very often. A quick rinse in summer is quite a different matter, using plain warm water or water to which a little body brace has been added, and many horses are washed, scraped and sponged every time they work in the summer, and then walked dry. You will find that it makes grooming much easier, though of course it does not do for circulation what brushing does. In any case, whenever caked sweat is a problem you will always want to sponge this off, taking special pains with the saddle mark, under the girth, around the ears and in the pastern area.

Some people object to seeing horses simply doused with a cold hose when they come in hot, and these same people probably hate taking cold showers themselves. However, it is widely practiced, and I have never heard of a problem that could be traced to it. Whether you use warm water or a cold hose for the summer bath, always be sure to walk the horse dry afterwards. You will know that he can safely be returned to the stall when the area between his front legs is dry. If you do not take pains to insure that the horse has cooled off inside as well as outside, he will probably break out again once he is in the stall.

9

Worming

ALL HORSES HAVE worms, and all horses should be wormed periodically whether there are visible signs of worm infestation or not. Obvious signs of worms are loss of weight, dull coat, pot belly, and digestive disturbances. Less obvious signals may be a necessity to feed more grain than usual to keep the horse's weight up, or a lack of energy. Worms can make the difference between a poor keeper and a good one; the fewer worms in a horse's system, the better he can digest his food and the more benefit he gets from it.

The severity of your worm problem will depend to a large extent on the number of horses you have, the amount of pasture available, and your stable management and hygiene program. Sometimes the care the horse received before you bought him can have a bearing on it, as a horse that has had heavy worm infestation may take years to fully recover from it.

To help you understand the problems of worms in horses without going into unnecessary detail, the problem is basically this: horses recycle worms through their bodies by their droppings. The worms go from grass to horse to manure back to grass, etc., etc., or begin the cycle in the horse and go to manure to grass (or bedding in the stall) and back to the horse. One of the reasons for keeping the stall cleaned is so the horse does not pick up as many worms from his manure in the bedding. In the pasture, worms go from manure to the grass, where they are picked up by the horse when he grazes, and are spread by the horses walking around. Rotating pasture breaks the cycle of the worm population.

You should always discuss the problem of worming with your vet, since there are five different kinds of worms, and the correct frequency of worming may vary with each horse and each stable. Your vet can give you the best advice about how and when to worm. He will determine whether your horse needs to be "tubed," in which the medicine is administered directly to the stomach, or whether you can use an oral medicine in the horse's feed.

Horses kept on pasture that is rotated regularly may need to be wormed only once or twice a year, whereas a horse that is always stabled may need it as often as every two or three months. Do not depend on over-the-counter worm medicines available in feed stores unless your vet specifically tells you to.

Do not neglect to worm your horses because he isn't showing any "signs" of worms. The benefit of worming is that it prevents the worm infestation from getting to the point where it causes damage to the system. By the time the horse is showing signs of worms, damage has already been done that may take months to heal. If there is any question in your mind, do not hesitate to take a manure sample and give it to your vet for analysis.

10

Teeth

SOME PEOPLE MAKE a big fuss about telling a horse's age by his teeth, and it's perfectly true that some vets and dealers who examine a great many horses acquire a considerable facility at it. As a practical matter, however, most self-styled experts are doing well if they can tell you whether the horse is young or old, and even people who get to look into many horses' mouths are often wrong by a couple of years.

Still, if you need an approximation of a horse's age and have no papers to refer to, your vet can probably give you the closest guess. It's much easier, however, to look at the horse's breeding or performance registration—Jockey Club, if he's a Thoroughbred, or Quarter Horse, Appaloosa, Morgan, Half-Thoroughbred or whatever. Sometimes a Thoroughbred is sold without his papers, but if he's ever been at the track you'll find an identification number tattooed inside his upper lip. In this code there is a letter with a four-digit number, and the system started with the letter A in 1945 and started repeating in 1971, so you can figure out the year in which the horse was foaled by simply running through the alphabet.

Obviously, teeth have a considerable importance quite aside from determining the age of a horse, because their condition has an immediate effect on the general health of the animal. A horse's teeth both grow and wear as he ages, and sharp edges can form over a period of years that can easily cut or irritate his mouth. When this happens the horse may go off his feed and start to lose weight, or he may get generally dull and cranky acting. These sharp edges can also result in an uneven bite which causes the horse to chew improperly, so he doesn't digest his grain completely. Other signs of tooth problems include fussing with the bit excessively, and chewing with the head cocked to one side.

When the horse develops these problems, he needs to have his teeth "floated," or filed. To check the horse's teeth, you will need two people. Tie the horse fairly short.

One person holds his mouth open, while the other one looks at his teeth and runs his hand along the grinding teeth in the back of the horse's mouth to check for rough edges.

Opening the horse's mouth to examine it. My left thumb is on the bars of his mouth where there are no teeth. To check for sharp edges I would pull the tongue over to one side to keep the mouth open, and have someone feel the teeth behind my hand.

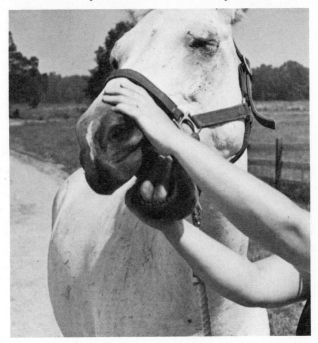

Often the gums or inside of the mouth where the teeth have been rubbing will be inflamed or discolored, also.

Standing beside the horse's head, reach under his neck and slip two fingers into his mouth in the space where the bit goes (the bars of the mouth), and open his mouth, much as you would do to bridle him. As he opens his mouth, grasp his tongue with your other hand and gently pull it over to one side, so that the horse will keep his mouth open to avoid biting it. Keep a firm grip on his lower jaw. The other person can now both help to keep the horse's head still, and quickly run his fingers along the teeth, reaching all the way into the back of the horse's mouth to check all the teeth behind the bars of the mouth, which are the grinding teeth. All this must be done quickly, for the horse won't stand still for long.

If the horse objects strenuously, you should wait and let the vet do it, as he has instruments for holding the horse's mouth open. When a vet or traveling tooth man floats teeth, he uses a file with a long handle to rasp the edges off the teeth, much as a dentist does.

Occasionally a horse will have trouble

cutting a tooth, or will get a tooth broken, knocked out, or displaced. If it doesn't seem to bother him, keep an eye on it, but the chances are that it will never get in the way. If the horse goes off his feed, or seems ill or unusually bad tempered, get the vet to check him. Sometimes an infected tooth can give a horse the symptoms of a cold or shipping fever, causing the glands under the jaw or at the throat to swell.

Stallions, geldings, and some mares will cut "tushes," sometimes called "wolf teeth," between the ages of four and five years. These teeth, which come in at the back of the bars of the mouth and in front of the molars in the back of the mouth, are longer and have a more rounded end than the other teeth. Occasionally a gelding will go through a long cranky spell until these teeth finally come in, much as people do with their wisdom teeth.

If your horse habitually fusses with the bit, carries his head to one side, becomes a sloppy eater or seems to chew oddly, you should suspect tooth problems. It is wise to have a vet check a horse's teeth yearly to prevent problems from arising from tooth trouble. This job can be done when you bring the vet out for the yearly vaccinations.

If you live in a horsey area, there may be an itinerant tooth man who goes from farm to farm, doing teeth and nothing else, and these specialists are usually excellent if you can locate one.

11

Inoculations

TETANUS IS A disease which most of us know about and customarily immunize our children against. We should take the same precaution with horses, as tetanus is more common in the horse than in any other domestic animal. The organism which causes tetanus is a common inhabitant of the horse and other herbivorous animals, and the disease is caused when a wound is contaminated and a chemical reaction is set up that produces the symptoms. Wounds may be infected at the time of infliction, or afterwards by soil contamination. Frequently the symptoms do not occur until after the wound has healed. Initial symptoms include a stiffness in the muscles, straddling gait, and slowness in eating. If the symptoms are diagnosed soon enough and "lock-jaw"—when the muscles go into spasm until the jaws cannot open—is avoided, the horse may recover. However, because immunization is available, tetanus can be prevented easily.

The veterinarian will give your horse two shots four to five weeks apart, which will confer immunity for a year. After a year a booster shot is given which protects the horse for two to three years.

If you are not sure if your horse has had a tetanus immunization, you should call the vet for a shot. The vet will also give a tetanus shot when castrating or operating on an animal, as tetanus is often contracted after castration (gelding).

If a mare in foal is given a tetanus shot late in her pregnancy, in addition to her regular immunization, the foal will be protected for two to three months, after which he should be given the regular immunization series.

The tetanus immunization is injected into a muscle, usually either in the neck or the triceps muscle, the fleshy muscle above the elbow of the horse.

The other major disease for which horses should be inoculated is equine encephalomyelitis or sleeping sickness, which has two strains, the one which is usually called domestic, and the Venezuelan strain, known as VEE. This disease, which is an inflammation of the brain, is spread by mosquitoes, and is usually fatal. The vet can give the horse a shot yearly to prevent these diseases.

Many people have had horses for years and have never had them inoculated, with no ill results. They are very, very lucky. Horses are like children, and need to be protected against diseases which can be fatal. It is much wiser to have the vet come out at least once a year to give inoculations, worm the horses, check the teeth, etc.

12

Common Illnesses

SOME TIME DURING your years as a horse owner, you will undoubtedly come into contact with one or more equine illnesses. In the best of stables things go wrong sometimes, and problems arise from feeding problems or chills that cause worry and vet bills.

Colic is perhaps the most common "illness" seen in horses. Actually colic is just a stomachache, but it can lead to complications, and it can be caused by the horse being "under the weather" from another illness. When a horse gets colic, he hurts. It may be caused by overeating, or by eating something that produced too much gas in the stomach and intestines. The horse reacts to colic by becoming restless, acting uncomfortable and walking around his stall. He may have a worried, anxious expression, he may keep turning his head around to look at his sides, or he may try to bite at his sides. He may also try to lie down and roll, trying to relieve the pain.

Colic is common in the horse, probably because of the small size of his stomach and the fact that a horse cannot vomit. Thus if he eats something that makes him sick, he must still pass it through the intestines. It is more common at night-time, and can be caused by an insufficient supply of water, irregularity in feeding, feeding a large amount of feed when the horse isn't used to it, or feeding a heavy amount of grain after a hard day's work, particularly if the horse was deprived of water during the day (such as after a horse show, a day of hunting, or a long trail ride.) Some horses are more prone to colic than others, particularly those with an extremely nervous disposition, and cribbers.

Colic can also be caused by moldy food, poor hay, soiled food (feed that has had a heavy infestation by mice or rats), by watering a horse that is very hot and sweaty (from work, not from the heat of the day), or by riding a horse directly after a full feeding. (Wait a full hour before working the horse above a walk.)

The first thing to do if you suspect your horse has colic is to remove his feed and water. If the weather is cold, it is wise to keep the horse warm and out of drafts, putting a light blanket on him if necessary. Put him in a stall, or small paddock, and keep him quiet. Most cases of colic are mild, and most cases recover without any treatment at all. Usually the most effective thing you can do for your horse is to keep him quiet and keep him from rolling, even if you have to lead him around to keep him up.

If you are worried that the horse may injure himself, or that he may have either a severe case of colic or possibly some digestive disturbance other than colic, or if he swells in the flanks and in the hollow just in front of the point of the hip, you should call the vet. In cases of flatulent colic, when the stomach and/or intestines become distended with gas, the vet may have to tap the bowel to let out the gas. Or he may give the horse a "drench," which is a medication given orally to ease the pain and gas of colic.

If you cannot reach the vet, and you feel a drench is necessary, you can mix a drench of either linseed oil and water (1 pint of linseed oil and 8 oz. of water) or a pint of linseed oil, 2 oz. of turpentine, and 8 oz. of water, and give it to the horse. A drench can be given in a coke bottle, if nothing else is available, or a plastic bottle such as is used for dish washing liquid, provided the soap is washed out thoroughly. Or you can use a turkey baster. To drench the horse, have someone hold his head as high up as you can get it, with his nose pointed upwards, and open his mouth and pour the drench down his throat.

When the horse has recovered from his colic, keep an eye on him for a few more hours. Give him water, but wait about 12 hours before you feed him. Try to figure out what caused the problem. If it is your feed, or your hay, do not give him any more of the same. Be more careful of how and when you feed, or how close to feeding you ride the horse. If the horse colicked after a hard day of showing or hunting, make a note to insure that he is watered more frequently during the day he is taken to such events, and make sure he is rested before eating in the evening following this type of work. Also, try to feed him earlier on the days he goes out for this, to give him time in the morning before work to digest his feed.

Founder is another problem that is fairly

common, and that is usually preventable. It is such a common term that many of us use it without fully understanding what it means, and we tend to assume that people know what it is even when they don't. Founder is sometimes called "fever in the feet," which gives you an idea of what it is like. It is an inflammation of the sensitive laminae of the hooves, which are layers of tissue in the hoof itself. Thus the term "laminitis." Founder is caused by congestion of blood in the feet of the horse, which causes these layers of tissue in the hoof to become extremely painful and swollen. The result is severe lameness, and if the condition is not treated or relieved, the hoof itself becomes misshapen from the pressure of the swollen tissues inside it. This causes the telltale "rings of founder" on the hooves of horses that have been foundered. Instead of coming down smoothly from the coronet to the ground, the front of the hoof seems to be wrinkled and bumpy, and the toe becomes long and the hoof appears concave.

Founder occurs most frequently in the front feet of the horse because most of the weight of the horse is supported by the front feet when the horse is standing still, and the blood supply to the front feet is greater and slower than that of the rear. Any condition which tends to encourage the congestion of the blood in the feet and legs may lead to founder. For instance, when a horse is exercised to the point where his heart is pounding, and he is very heated up, his circulation increases and his body temperature rises. If the horse is watered in this condition, the effect of the cool water is to immediately reduce both his body temperature and the circulation of blood in his body. This can result in the blood "pooling" in the legs and feet, because the gravity of the earth pulls blood down the legs, but the slowed circulation cannot pull it back up. Founder can result, particularly if the horse is allowed to stand, or is put into his stall. Thus, when the horse is hot from exertion, water him sparingly, and walk him until he has cooled down, to keep the flow of circulation even and to prevent founder.

Another situation that favors founder is when the horse is fed an amount of food much larger or richer than he is used to, particularly when he has been in a stall all day or night, or for several days without adequate exercise. Standing in a stall for long periods of time tend to make the legs "stock up," or swell below the knees and

hocks, due to poor circulation. The horse
does not move around enough to push the
blood through the legs and feet, so gravity
makes it collect in the feet. When the horse
is fed, particularly a large meal, his circula-
tory system must send an increased amount
of blood to the abdomen for digestion to
take place. This increase of the supply of
blood to the digestive system decreases the
supply and flow of blood to the legs, and
aggravates the situation of slow or poor circulation. Thus the congestion which causes
founder can be set up.

Any condition which causes disruption
of the circulation in the legs and favors
congestion of blood in the feet can cause
founder, so it is difficult to describe all
of the things that can cause it. In general,
an imbalance of feed and work (too much
work and not enough feed, or too much
feed and not enough work, or too much
feed or water to a hot horse) is the most
common cause of founder.

It should also be remembered that once a
horse is foundered he is much more likely
to get it again, and some horses become
chronic cases. Foundered horses should be
kept out of situations in which they must be
stabled for long hours, if possible.

Large horses with very small feet, and very small ponies, particularly very fat ones, are more prone to founder, and any severely overweight horse or pony is very prone to it.

The symptoms of founder are usually clear-cut and easy to observe. The horse becomes extremely sore on whichever feet are affected. (Sometimes only one forefoot is affected.) The horse will be very lame, and will exhibit discomfort even when standing still, by becoming restless and sweaty, shifting his weight back and forth from foot to foot, stretching out in the front, and generally acting uncomfortable. His heels and feet will feel hot to the touch. (To check this, feel all four feet, coronets and pasterns and compare them.) In severe cases the horse may even lie down. In mild cases, however, there may be soreness as if the horse had bruised his feet on gravel, with little heat, and only a small amount of discomfort.

Because founder is caused by a vascular imbalance, treatment consists of trying to relieve the animal's pain and restoring the proper flow of blood to and from the legs. The first thing to do is to take away the horse's feed and water until the discomfort is past and the horse is back to normal, to prevent aggravation of the condition. Ideally, the best thing to do would be to roll the horse over on his back with his feet up in the air, but unfortunately that is rather impractical. If the horse will lie down, however, let him, as this is probably the best position for him. Make sure that you roll him over to the other side several times a day, however, to prevent dangerous congestion in other areas of his body.

If the horse will not lie down, standing him in either cold or hot water, or alternating them, is beneficial in relieving the pain. Standing the horse in a cold stream or creek is often the handiest way to do this. In severe cases, the veterinarian can pare away the hoof to allow the blood to drain, and then pack the hoof to stop the flow. Walking the horse would aid in restoring the proper circulation, but it would seem cruel to attempt this, due to the extreme pain founder causes.

Whenever the horse is seriously lame or sore on his forefeet, and no other specific reason for it can be found, it is wise to assume it is at least a mild case of founder, and treat it as such.

The other most common illnesses of horses that you are likely to come across are so close in symptoms that I will discuss them together. These diseases are called "shipping fever" and "strangles," and although many people use the terms interchangeably, they are two separate illnesses. In fact, strangles is often called shipping fever by mistake. However, shipping fever is the less serious of the two. Shipping fever is equine influenza. It is also called pink eye, and is common in young horses and those that have been moved into new surroundings, hence the term "shipping fever." The chief symptoms of shipping fever are listlessness and runny eyes and nose. The symptoms occur rather suddenly, and the horse becomes feverish, loses his appetite, becomes depressed and hangs his head. The conjunctiva (white lining around the eyes) become red and inflamed looking, the eyes and nose run profusely, and the glands may swell at the throttle. In severe cases swelling may also occur in the lower legs and under the belly.

Strangles, like shipping fever, causes the animal to be feverish and listless. But strangles is a streptococcus infection, and the identifying symptoms are nasal discharge and pronounced swellings at the throttle and under the jaw. The horse exhibits difficulty in swallowing, and may lose his appetite completely. Generally the swellings abscess and break spontaneously, although they sometimes must be lanced (opened with a knife).

Both shipping fever and strangles are extremely contagious, and a person handling an infected horse should change his clothes and wash thoroughly before handling one that is not. Because of the likelihood of a newly arrived horse carrying one of these diseases, it is recommended that a new horse be isolated from the other horses in the stable for at least two weeks before he is turned in with them.

Both diseases, if left untreated, can develop complications which can be fatal. Pneumonia often occurs with untreated cases of shipping fever, and strangles can develop into pneumonia, or abscesses can form in other parts of the body, including the intestines, which is fatal. In addition, strangles can lead to permanent damage to the larynx and/or lungs of the horse.

Treatment for both diseases consists of massive doses of antibiotics, which the veterinarian will give in a series of shots. If you have some experience with horses, the vet may show you how to give intramuscular shots so you can give your own antibiotics, which will save him time and you money.

Once a horse has recovered from strangles, he has a lifelong immunity from it, but a horse can get shipping fever more than one time.

If your horse shows signs of a cold and his glands swell, it is wise to call the vet, as it is probably either shipping fever or strangles. Leaving these diseases untreated can endanger a horse's life, or may impair his soundness for life if he recovers. If one horse in a stable contracts one of these diseases, the vet will probably recommend giving all the horses in the stable antibiotics to prevent or control an outbreak.

13

How to Tell When
Your Horse Is Sick

SINCE HORSES CAN'T tell us in words when they are ill, or injured, we have to figure it out from the way they act. As with people, illnesses cause symptoms, some of which we learn to recognize as being signs of specific problems, some of which are general symptoms and tell us only that something is wrong. In other words, the horse will act differently when he is sick.

But how do you tell when the horse is really sick, or just in a bad mood? First of all, the fact that a horse is in a "bad mood" may mean that something is wrong. Horses are rarely like people who just get into moods where they are stubborn or un-cooperative just for the heck of it. There may be times when a mare is more irritable and nervous because of being in heat, but these changes are usually different from and more obvious than symptoms of illness.

When a horse is coming down with something, or is actually ill, usually the first thing that happens is a loss of appetite. If your horse is "off his feed" (a lack of interest in food, ranging from not finishing a meal to totally ignoring it) for more than twenty-four hours, he is probably sick. Horses do not stop eating for no good reason. If you notice him being less hungry than usual, or not hungry at all, keep an eye on him, and look for other symptoms.

Another sign of illness, particularly of fever, is a general listlessness. When a normally active horse suddenly becomes tired-acting, standing around with his head down and not reacting as usual to other horses or people, he is probably sick. A dull, uninterested look in his eye when he is usually bright-eyed is also an indication.

On the other hand, a horse that is normally quiet and docile that suddenly becomes nervous, jumpy and lively should be looked at closely. Discomfort may make a quiet horse more restless, trying to relieve the pain by moving around.

A change for the worse in the condition of the horse's coat, when feeding and work schedules do not change, may also be an indication of illness. It is also a common symptom of worm infestation, and a stool specimen examined by a vet can determine whether it is worms or something more serious.

In general, any abrupt change in the horse's actions, appearance or appetite should be regarded as a sign of possible illness. More obvious signs include discharge from eyes or nose, coughing, diarrhea, cloudy or odd colored or smelling urine, abrupt change in the condition or texture of the stools without a change in diet, sweating in the stall for no apparent reason, etc.

If any one of these symptoms or any combination of them occurs for more than twenty-four hours, the horse has something wrong with him, for usually none of these things occurs for very long unless the horse is ill. A runny eye may be due to a little dust, but if it continues for more than a day or two, it is probably more serious. The horse may have diarrhea because he accidentally ate an irritating weed, but if it persists the horse may dehydrate. This is one reason for handling and checking the horse every day, whether you ride him or not, and even if he is out at pasture and you are not feeding him grain.

Vets, as we all know, are expensive. And

since most of us don't want to spend any more money on our horses than we can help, we don't want to call the vet unnecessarily, any more than he wants to come out and look at all kinds of inconsequential things. It is therefore helpful if we can judge when it is necessary to call him, and when we can take care of the problem ourselves.

The symptoms mentioned above are usually the first indications that something is wrong, but they are also usually corroborated by more objective tests of pulse, respiration and temperature.

The horse's normal resting pulse declines with age, but should not exceed 60 beats per minute for a mature animal. (The easiest place to take his pulse is on the big artery that crosses the jawbone in the cleft of his throat.) Normal respiration is twelve to thirteen breaths a minute, or slightly more in very hot weather. Normal temperature is from 99.5 to just over 100 degrees, and anything over 102 indicates fever. Temperatures should be taken rectally with a lubricated veterinary thermometer to which a string can be attached, to eliminate any danger of losing the thermometer in the rectum.

When you discuss a problem with your vet it will help him if you describe these symptoms as well as the more general ones. Temperatures of over 103 are serious ones, and those above 104 require very prompt attention.

A horse in the course of knocking around the pasture and stable will end up with various little cuts and scrapes. He may also develop sores or galls from ill-fitting tack, step on something sharp and puncture his foot, get in a fight and get bitten or kicked, or get chased through the fence and get cut. Injuries are usually easy to detect, and we can usually tell if the vet is needed. Any deep puncture wounds, particularly in the area of the feet or lower legs, or arterial bleeding require the attention of the vet. Even if the horse has had his tetanus shot, there is much danger of infection. Cuts that gape open and obviously require stitching need the vet. Any lameness severe enough to cause the horse to rest or raise the foot, or that persist over a period of time, usually require professional attention. In short, any injury that results in a drastic cut, swelling, soreness or lameness should be seen to by a vet, until the owner has sufficient knowledge and experience to care for them. (See chapter on Injuries.)

When a horse is ill, it is often harder to tell when and if the vet is really needed. If the horse gets down and cannot get up again, and is not cast, the vet is drastically needed, and should be called as soon as possible and told it is an emergency. If the horse is off his feed because of something he ate, the problem may pass all by itself and calling the vet may be a waste of time and money, but on the other hand, if the horse is really sick, a delay in treatment may be serious.

For instance, a few years ago we had a mare that was a very easy keeper, who suddenly quit eating. We looked her over and couldn't find anything, other than that she didn't seem quite her chipper self, and turned her back out in the pasture without worrying too much about it. But a few days later, she was still not eating, and had lost a noticeable amount of weight. We called the vet, and he discovered that somehow this mare had cut or scraped the inside of her throat, possibly by swallowing a stick or some other sharp object. She had a torn, and now, infected throat. In spite of the vet's efforts, she died. If we had called the vet right away instead of waiting, he might have been able to control the infection with antibiotics. Our delay, caused because we couldn't find any obvious symptoms of illness, cost us a good horse. If a horse refuses to eat or drink, or both, for more than twenty-four hours, call the vet.

Horses, like people, get colds. Some go away in a few days, but some hang on and on and go into more serious problems. If the horse has runny eyes and nose, but otherwise seems normal, keep an eye on him. If he develops a cough, don't ride him, and watch him more closely. If he then loses his appetite, gets listless, or extra restless, or develops swollen glands, call the vet. A series of antibiotics given at the onset of shipping fever or strangles may insure that these diseases affect the horse only slightly, and a persistent cough in a horse should be treated by a vet. It may be a cold, but if the cough persists it may be a sign of more serious trouble, such as heaves.

Heaves is a chronic condition which is similar to emphysema in humans. It produces asthma-like symptoms (shortness of breath, coughing, etc.) and reduces the ability of the horse to work. In most cases it can be controlled or improved by special diets (beet pulp) and antihistamines given in the feed.

If the horse's eyes begin to run, it may be

the onset of a cold or it may be an allergy, but if one eye only runs, he may have something in it. If it does not clear up in a day or two, or if the discharge turns cloudy, the eye turns cloudy or seems to get a film over it, if the lining of the eye turns red, or if the eye swells closed, consider it to be possibly serious. You can wash the eye with a mild boric acid solution and gently try to see if anything is lodged in the eye. An infection in the eye can lead to blindness. Worse, the problem may be an attack of moon blindness (periodic opthalmia) which will require the vet's attention.

In general, give the problem *some* time to solve itself, but don't wait too long. If symptoms of illness last for more than one full day, or get worse instead of better, call the vet.

In emergencies, if you can't reach the vet, your blacksmith may be able to give you some advice.

14

Care of the Sick Horse

IF YOUR HORSE is sick, but you do not know specifically what is wrong with him, you can do some general things to make him more comfortable. You can put him in his stall, or if the problem is in the legs or you otherwise think he should be able to exercise, in a small paddock, if the weather is good. You can put a blanket or sheet on him to keep him warm. Unless the problem is either colic or founder, give him plenty of fresh water. If it is either of these two things, withhold food and water until you have either talked to the vet for advice or all symptoms have disappeared. If the horse has a cold or other illness that is not related to colic, keep him warm and dry and give a laxative diet, checking with the vet for a recipe.

Do not ride a horse that you think may be sick. Whatever may be wrong with him will be aggravated by riding. Mild exercise may be helpful, but it should be in the form of leading or longeing. Do not expect the horse to carry both his illness and you.

If the horse has a cough that persists beyond the usual clearing of the throat, do not ride him until it goes away or is treated. Check your hay to see if it is dusty. If it is, sprinkling it lightly with water will help it until you can replace it with good hay.

Do not turn a sick horse out with the others, and do not let them sniff noses over the stall doors. Don't use the same equipment on a healthy horse that you used on a sick one without disinfecting it. The illness may be contagious. The extra excitement of being in contact with another horse may aggravate an illness.

When the horse recovers from an illness, it is a good idea to disinfect the stall. This includes washing the walls with a strong disinfectant, and cleaning the floor and sprinkling it heavily with lime. After the stall has dried and aired out, sweep up the extra lime and bed the stall down again with all fresh bedding. If sawdust or shavings were used for bedding, they should be removed from the stall after a sick horse has used it, and replaced with fresh.

15

Injuries

YOUR HORSE WILL probably get injured more often than he gets sick, although most of the injuries will probably be minor cuts and scrapes. Even minor cuts, however, can become serious if neglected.

Cuts or abrasions that do not actually break the skin, such as galls from ill-fitting tack, kicks and bites that take the hair off but do not draw blood, can be treated with a salve or Vaseline. They usually give no trouble, although if they are near a joint or sensitive area, they should be kept moist so the dry skin does not crack. If a gall has been caused by the tack, replace whatever piece of equipment caused it, or pad it to keep it from rubbing again. Galls on the withers mean the saddle presses too hard on this sensitive spot, and continued use may cause a "fistula."

A fistula is an abscess which is caused by
bacteria acting in a bruise or wound on or
near the withers or the poll. (One on the
poll is called "poll evil.") A fistula may
render a horse unridable for months, as it is
difficult to cure, particularly if it is left untreated for a time. Any lump, swelling, or
hot spots in the area of the withers should
be checked by a vet. If it is caught soon
enough, a fistula can be cured by injections
of antibiotics. However, if it is neglected, or
aggravated, it will become an open sore.
The horse should not be ridden with a
saddle until any sores or galls are gone from
the back and girth area. No amount of padding will make a saddle fit to put on a galled
or sore back, for it does not keep the saddle
from hurting when the rider's weight is
added.

Cuts, scrapes, and particularly rope burns
located around the pasterns and fetlocks
should be tended with special care, as they
are easily infected and often cause lameness.

When treating a cut near the eye, make
sure that the salve you use will not irritate
the eye if it is accidentally rubbed in.

Cuts that break the skin require more
careful consideration. Any cut that draws

blood should be treated, however small it may be. If the horse has not had his tetanus shot, one should be administered. Most wounds stop bleeding spontaneously, but if the horse has a cut that does not stop by itself, a pressure bandage can be applied.

If the cut is not on the legs, a hand bandage can be used. Using a folded towel or other clean rag, pinch the edges of the wound together and place the cloth over the wound, pressing *firmly* for as long a period of time as you can, releasing for rest periods, until the bleeding has stopped. If the wound is spurting but not arterial, and pressure does not stop the bleeding, alum or styptic powder applied directly in the wound should stop it.

If the wound is on the leg, a pressure wrap can be used. For this you will need a piece of gauze or a Telfa pad to cover the wound, roll gauze to wrap it (optional), a soft, clean towel to wrap around this, and an elastic bandage. As bleeding acts as a cleansing agent, it is not necessary to disinfect a wound before applying a pressure bandage to stop the bleeding. Cover the wound with the gauze pad, making sure any flaps of skin are in the right place and the wound is somewhat closed. Then wrap the

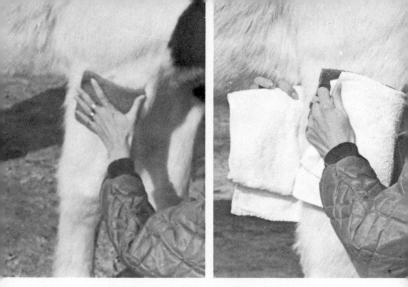

A pressure bandage should be applied to a wound that is bleeding freely. 1. First, close the wound by pressing a clean, soft cloth on it. 2. Then wrap an absorbent towel around it to absorb blood and distribute pressure more evenly. 3. Keep your hand pressing tightly so the bandage won't slip down or open the wound. 4. Anchor the bandage tightly, since it is difficult to keep a bandage up on this part of the leg, a common site of wounds.

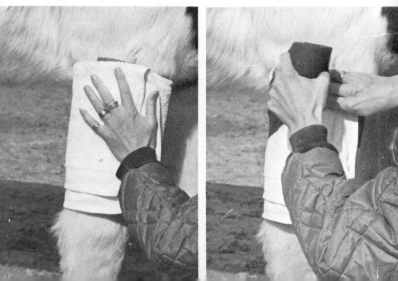

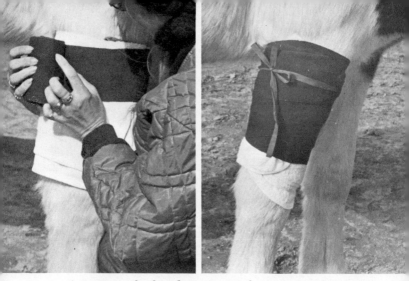

5, 6. *Wrap the bandage as tightly as you can to stop the bleeding. Check it after 15 to 20 minutes, and remove it after a half-hour, being careful not to break the wound open again. The wound can be treated once bleeding has been stopped.*

roll of gauze to hold the pad in place, following with the toweling wrapped around the leg to absorb the blood. Finish by wrapping the elastic bandage *snugly* around the leg, starting just above the wound and working downwards past it and then back up over it a few inches. If the horse moves around while you are trying to bandage him, have someone hold his opposite foot up, or, if you are alone, tie the foot up by tying a rope around the pastern and running a loop around the horse's girth.

When you are sure the bleeding has
stopped (usually in about fifteen minutes),
slowly unwrap the bandage and take it off.
Now you can cleanse the wound. I have
found that the best cleaner is hydrogen peroxide, the kind that you use around the
house anyway. It can be used anywhere except around the eyes. Its foaming action
washes the wound out. It can best be administered by soaking a piece of soft cotton
with it and squeezing it into the wound. If
you don't have peroxide, any disinfectant
that is mild will do, even Listerine. Do not
use alcohol, as it will damage the tissues.

After the wound is cleaned, you should
decide whether you can treat it yourself or
whether you should call the vet to stitch it.
If the wound is gaping open, or if it is more
than about half an inch deep, you should
probably get the vet to look at it. Wounds
like this usually get infected, and the vet
will want to give the horse an antibiotic
shot. If you decide to call the vet, you will
want to keep the wound from drying out
before he gets there. To do this, put a
water-soluble salve on the wound. *Never*
put Vaseline on a wound before the vet
treats it—it will prevent him from cleaning it and getting a good look at it. Vaseline

will not wash off, and it can keep dirt in a wound as well as out.

If a wound does not begin to improve within a day or two, or if it looks worse (runny, inflamed, filling with pus, etc.), it is probably getting infected. Repeated cleansing with peroxide may cure it, but it is probably wiser to call the vet and have him treat it. Remember, too, that repeated doses of peroxide may make the hair fall out around and below a cut, and may make the skin turn pale, but this is not necessarily a sign of infection.

If the horse has a puncture wound in the foot, first wash the foot by soaking it in a bucket of water. Pour peroxide (or Chlorox) over the sole of the foot, dry it off, and then pour iodine into the puncture. If the puncture is deep or large, you may need to pack it with a towel and make a foot bandage. A feed bag cut in half, slipped over the hoof and tied above the fetlock joint will make a good temporary one. Then call the vet, as puncture wounds in the feet are serious.

When treating wounds, stay calm. Remember that a healthy horse can lose up to three gallons of blood (and this looks like ten) without serious danger to his health. Don't hesitate to call the vet if you even suspect a cut may need stitches, as a delay of even a day or two can sometimes mean that the vet is unable to stitch because of the wound's drying out or swelling.

16

Lameness

POSSIBLY THE MOST common problem related to the horse's health is lameness.
Sometimes a horse will go lame for a few
days and you never do know for sure what
caused it, or even which leg or legs he was
lame on.

When you notice your horse is lame, the
first thing to do is to try to locate the site of
the problem. Sometimes it is obvious: there
will be a swelling, or a cut. But more often
there is really nothing at all that you can
see.

Get someone to lead the horse for you, or
put him on the longe line. First watch him
move out at a walk. Does he actually limp,
bobbing his head and noticeably favoring
one leg as it hits the ground, or does he
just look sore to you, taking unusually small

strides? Does he stride the same distance with each leg, or is he stepping short with one leg, or with both hind legs?

After you watch him walk, trot the horse. Sometimes if the lameness is slight, it will be quite hard to see at a walk, but will show up at the trot. Sometimes you can't even see it then, but if you ride the horse, you can feel a difference in the horse's gaits especially on one lead or diagonal. If this is the case, the problem may be muscular in the legs or in the back, and you should not ride him. When the horse trots, his head may bob up and down, which he will not do if he is sound.

When you watch the horse move out, first try to decide if the lameness is in the front or hind legs. Look at the hind legs first, as lameness is often easier to detect here. Is the horse tracking as usual, or is he stepping shorter with one leg, or with both? If he is taking shorter steps with both hind legs, he may be sore on all four feet, or if he is barefoot behind, he may be sore behind because his feet have worn down too short. Then again, he may be lame in front, and is stepping short in the back to take the weight off his forehand. If he is taking short steps with one hind leg, he is probably lame in that leg, but he could be lame in the diagonal front leg.

If the horse is traveling normally in the rear, or if you think he may be moving strangely but you can find no signs of injury in the hind legs (after feeling both hips, stifles, hocks, fetlocks, pasterns and coronets, and examining the hooves for heat, swellings or cuts) the problem should be in the front. If the horse is moving poorly, and you can't find anything, assume that the problem is in the front, for it is unusual for a horse to be sore in the rear and sound in the front, unless he has a stifle or hock problem. If the horse seems to drag one hind leg, or won't bring it forward very far, check the hip and stifle very carefully. Compare the joints on both sides by looking at the horse from the rear as well as the side. Feel both sides to compare for heat. Call the vet if the hip or stifle is displaced noticeably.

Tendon problems are not common in the rear legs, although sickle hocks (when the leg slants forward from the hock down, giving the joint too much angle) may predispose to curbs (a lump on the back of the hock just below the point of the hock). A soft, hot swelling on the outside of the hock is a bog spavin (also called thoroughpin), which causes lameness when it happens.

A hard knot, also with heat, on the inside of the hock joint may be a bone spavin ("jack") which is more serious. To test a horse for a spavin, hold the hind leg so the fetlock joint is as close to the stifle as you can get it, while someone holds the horse who can lead him at a trot. Hold the leg up tight for one to two minutes. Then let go, and have the person lead the horse off at a trot immediately. If the horse has a spavin, he will be noticeably lame after this test. If you think the horse is spavined, it is a good idea to call the vet. He can assess the situa-

Checking for a spavin. Hold the horse's leg up as high as you can for as long as you can (up to two minutes), then drop it and jog him immediately. If he has a spavin, this will make his lameness very conspicuous.

tion and give advice on how to treat it and how long you will have to rest the horse.

If you are satisfied that the problem is not in the rear, then begin to watch the front. Watch the horse's head at the trot. If it is nodding, the horse is favoring one side, as it does not normally nod at a trot. It is sometimes difficult to tell which leg is sore by watching the head, but remember that the head goes *up* when the sore leg hits the ground, because the horse is trying to throw his weight off it. Sometimes it is hard to keep up with the rhythm of the movement, and it is always wise to check both front legs and feet equally well, as you may be looking at the wrong leg in the first place.

Starting at the neck, feel all the way down the neck, through the shoulder and down the leg. A sore neck can make a horse lame, because the muscles that pull the front legs forward run all the way up the horse's neck to his poll. (This is why a good neck is so important to a horse's action.) Check for lumps, swellings, bruises, heat, cuts, etc. Remember that a cut or bruise on the knee may swell at the fetlock, as the fluid settles.

If the lameness is well defined, and makes the horse wince, it may be seated in the hoof. If it is a matter of taking irregular strides, it may be muscular and located in the shoulder. If the horse seems to "give" on one leg, as if he cannot bear weight on it, it may be a tendon problem. Most tendon difficulties are visible. To check a tendon, first feel the tendon while the horse is standing, comparing it with the other one. Check for swelling and heat. The tendon

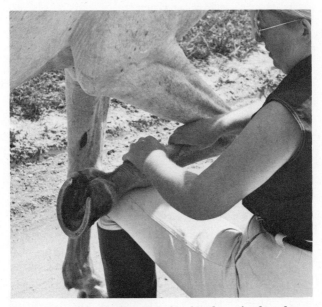

Checking the tendon. With the horse's leg lying across your leg, you can examine the slack tendon for bumps, heat or swelling.

should be hard, cool and smooth. Hard lumps may be old injuries that have healed. After you have felt it while the foot is down, pick up the horse's hoof and lay the cannon bone across your knee. (See picture.) With the leg relaxed, feel the tendon. It should feel loose but still hard and smooth. Look primarily for heat, as injury here produces congestion of blood, which causes heat.

If the problem cannot be located above the fetlock, feel the joint carefully, and then feel down the pastern and the coronary band. If the problem is in the hoof, the coronet may be hot. Again, compare it with the other hoof. You may be surprised to feel the heat in the one you weren't checking! If you can't find signs of anything at all, the problem is probably in the hoof, possibly a bruised sole.

To check the hoof, first clean and wash it so that you can check for small punctures or nail wounds. Push on the soft part of the heel, and tap the heel with something hard to see if he reacts. Feel just at or above the heel where the hair grows for a pulse beat. Normally the pulse cannot be felt in the heel, but if there is an injury in the hoof area the congestion will cause a pulse to be felt.

Go over the frog and sole carefully for

punctures. If the frog is badly infected with thrush, the lameness may be a result of that. Douse the hoof with thrush remedy (Chlorox can be used) and consult the blacksmith or vet.

If you find no thrush and no punctures, and there are no cracks in the hoof wall that could be causing the lameness, tap the sole of the hoof with a hammer or squeeze it with a hoof tester to see if the horse winces. Then do the other foot the same way. If he flinches on just one foot, then he probably is bruised on that foot. If he flinches on both front feet, try the hind feet. He may be the kind of horse that flinches easily. If he reacts on just the front feet, he may be bruised on both, or he may have a mild case of founder.

If the horse has a lameness that you just can't seem to pinpoint, it may be a good idea to assume that he has a mild case of founder, and treat him accordingly. Cut his grain ration in half, soak his feet in cold water, and keep an eye on him for a few days. Usually founder causes stocking up in the legs, and definite heat in the coronary area, but sometimes in a mild case lameness is the only sign. And no matter what the problem is, the founder treatment won't do any harm.

If a horse has a lameness that comes and goes with the same symptoms, and particularly if he points a forefoot to rest it when lame, the vet should be called in to check the horse. Recurring lameness may be a case of chronic founder, or it could be navicular disease. Navicular disease is a progressive degeneration of the bones within the hoof, and it eventually renders the horse unfit for work of any kind.

To summarize, try to find the site of the lameness by checking all four legs carefully. Check the forefeet carefully for punctures, cracks, and thrush. This may prevent you from missing a small cut or puncture that may develop into a major infection. Remember, a horse limps because it hurts, so don't treat lameness as minor. If your horse goes lame while you are riding, get off and lead him home. If a stabled horse goes lame, he should be exercised at a walk on a longe line, hot walker (machine that turns like a merry-go-round to which the horses are tied for exercise), or turned into a small paddock for exercise unless the vet recommends otherwise. Tendon problems can be treated with liniments if they are not serious. It is usually wise to call the vet and ask him for advice for tendon or foot problems.

17

Special Care of the Very Young or Very Old Horse

HORSES THAT ARE either too young to ride or too old need special care. They have special problems which regular horse care may not make allowances for.

When a foal is born, he has a specific genetic potential; that is, his parentage has given him certain characteristics. If he is cared for properly when he is growing up, and trained correctly, he will probably reach his potential — become as good a horse as his bloodlines permit. But if the foal does not get enough food, and the right kind of feed, his body will not develop as much as it could, and his growth will be stunted.

A foal's natural food during the first six months of his life is his mother's milk, plus grazing. If a mare and foal are pastured in a lush pasture, one that keeps the mare fat and shiny even after foaling, then it should be enough to keep the foal until weaning time. However, the average horse owner probably doesn't have this type of facility, as the breeding farms do. If your mare and foal do not have this much pasture, or none at all, then the foal needs to be fed grain and hay as soon as he will eat it. He will probably begin eating his mother's feed without a couple of weeks of birth, and when he gets two to three months old he should be given his own ration of grain.

By the time a foal is weaned, he should be getting as much grain and hay as he will clean up in the time it takes his mother to eat her grain. At this age it is practically impossible to overfeed, as the foal will not eat enough to make himself sick. If the foal has been raised on pasture, he should be started on grain and hay a month prior to weaning, so he will be used to it when the dam is taken away.

When the foal is weaned, you can keep grain in front of him all the time, if possible, to make sure he is getting enough. This is particularly important at this time because the upset of weaning will cause him to lose weight. Usually the best way to do it is to put 2 to 4 pounds of grain in the box in the morning (whether the foal is kept in a stall or small paddock), and check it around noon. If the foal has eaten it all, add another 2 pounds and check it again in the afternoon. Most horse foals will be eating somewhere in the neighborhood of 8 to 12 pounds of grain a day by the time they are eight months old, with hay if there is no pasture. Even with pasture, the foal should be fed grain. Several good prepared feeds designed specially for foals are on the market, and I strongly recommend feeding one of these rather than plain sweet stock. The added vitamins, minerals, and alfalfa meal definitely aid a foal's development.

When the foal is a yearling (by months, not using the Jan. 1 date), he can be put on regular sweet feed, unless he still needs special care. If you buy a weanling that has been neglected, for instance, you may want to continue the special feed until he has really come back to good health.

Care should be taken not to let a colt lose condition between one and two years. This is the year when most colts are turned out or forgotten, while the owner is waiting for him to get old enough to ride. But this year is as important as the first year, and it is now that the colt should be gotten into peak health and good condition for riding.

The horse that is very old may present

some problems in care, too. A horse in his late teens or twenties, that is no longer fit for riding, or that is showing signs of old age, should be treated carefully. Often a horse like this will begin to lose weight, lose the bloom to his coat and muscle tone, and generally go downhill. More often than not, this happens only because his age causes changes in his teeth and digestive system. The best thing that you can do for a "retired" horse is to turn him out to pasture in an area that is not too hilly or rough, and that has good shelter. The old horse will need to be wormed at least as often as the ones that are ridden. His teeth should be checked twice a year for problems if possible. If there is little pasture, or if the horse does not stay healthy on the pasture, then he should be fed the most easily chewed feed you can find. We feed our 32-year-old mare the prepared colt feed, because the pellets are small and easily chewed, and she needs the extra nutrients. If the horse's teeth are worn very much, you may have to chop the hay for him also.

Just because a horse is old, do not neglect his feet, teeth or inoculations. With a foal, or horse under two years old, make sure his feet are trimmed regularly by a good blacksmith. Many leg problems can be avoided by good trimming early, and a horse can become crippled if his feet are allowed to grow too long when he is young.

Part III

HORSE HANDLING

18

How the Horse Thinks

THE MOST IMPORTANT thing to remember about a horse's mind is that his first loyalty is to the person who feeds him. Therefore, if you are not the person who regularly feeds him, but are nevertheless the one who rides him, you will not necessarily have his full attention and respect. In order that the horse attach some feelings for you, other than dread at the sight of you, it is necessary that you provide at least part of his food. Make it a habit to give him one of his meals after your ride. If you feed him, he will like you, and he will look forward to seeing you.

The second thing that horses respond to as far as people are concerned is comfort. They react to things that make them feel good in a favorable way. They like to be groomed; to an extent they enjoy being petted. Most important, they like to be as comfortable as possible when they are being ridden or handled, and they react adversely to pain.

The third thing to remember about horses is that they frighten easily. As animals go, the horse is fairly poorly protected from harm. His natural weapons of self-defense are his speed and his hard hooves. Because he is limited in his ability to fight, and escape is not always possible, the horse compensates by being extremely wary of danger.

This does not mean that all horses are nervous and jumpy. It merely means that they are capable of being this way, it is their instinct. Whether or not they act unusually nervous depends in a large part on how they are treated. If a horse is not certain of his safety, is often put into frightening or confusing situations, and receives pain from these circumstances, then he will use his natural instincts and become nervous and excitable. If, however, he is rarely hurt and rarely frightened, he will suppress his natural fears and become a calm, reasonable character, as we know most horses to be.

Horses are frightened by loud or sudden noises. Car backfires, gunshots, etc., will spook him. A horse when frightened reacts predictably. First, he attempts to run, since

his greatest protection from danger is his
speed. If he is in a position where he cannot
run (in a stall, for instance) he will whirl
and kick out, his second best weapon being
his hard hooves and strong hind legs. If he
cannot turn around (if he is tied) he may
rear, and possibly strike out with his forefeet. Thus, a horse will usually shy, bolt
forward, or at least crouch in readiness to
run when he hears a loud, sudden noise. He
will also react to any suspicious noise, such
as a rustle in the leaves that could be a
snake. If the horse is tied, he may kick out
at a noise behind him.

Horses are often frightened by strange
looking objects. This means either things
that they have never seen before, or things
they have seen but that have changed, or
have been moved, etc. Sometimes it seems
that they consider an object strange if they
see it from a different angle or in a different
light. This explains why a horse may shy at
a rock going out but not coming back. I also
believe that some horses become habitual
shiers, because they learn that sudden
movement may unseat the rider and get him
to take the horse home.

Horses are usually frightened, at least at
first, by strange animals. This may include

people, since people are just another kind
of animal to a horse. If a horse has reason to
believe that people may hurt him, he may
be more afraid of them than any other kind.
Generally horses will react to the sudden
appearance of, or even the gradual sight of
dogs, cows, deer, pigs, small children or
even other horses, although the fear usually
turns into a lively interest once they recognize the animal and realize that it will
not harm them.

A horse that has been attacked by a dog,
however, may retain a lifelong fear of dogs,
and some horses are naturally suspicious of
any biting animal regardless of whether or
not they have ever been attacked. Apparently some horses have a more pronounced self-preservation instinct than
others. And some horses, like some people,
are just naturally more nervous than others,
and will frighten more easily and react more
violently when scared.

Sometimes a horse's reactions to fear may
resemble, and in fact overlap, his sense of
anger. Some horses develop behavior which
closely parallels anger in people, and which
is probably a self-protective instinct in-
stigated by fear. A horse that bites, kicks, or
otherwise exhibits what is usually called

bad temper, or bad disposition, is using habits caused originally by fear and continued partly out of fear of punishment and partly out of habit. A horse startled in his stall may kick out in fear, and the rider, in turn frightened by the kick, runs out and leaves the horse alone. The horse has then learned that kicking relieves him of attention by the rider, and he learns that if he doesn't want to be disturbed while eating, or if he doesn't want to be ridden, he can kick at the rider and be left alone. What originated as fear became a bad habit. Bad disposition in horses is, I believe, almost entirely taught. There are a few horses that seem to be born mean, that are hard to handle and ill-tempered from the day they are born, but I think they are fairly rare.

Generally, sensible, kind treatment results in reasonable behavior in the horse, provided the good treatment is tempered by strictness in the obedience to certain rules. Horses should not be allowed to kick, bite, or otherwise do things that are likely to result in injury or inconvenience to either them or their owner. This rule must be enforced absolutely. The owner should see to it that the horse is never allowed to break the no-harm rule. The horse must never

learn that he can get away with hurting people, and as we all know, the wrong lessons
seem to be the quickest learned. We must
be careful to train the horse, not have him
train us.

By the same token, the owner must follow
the rule which says he must never inten-
tionally hurt the horse except in the manner
of just and immediate punishment. A horse
should never be hurt unless he has broken a
rule, committed a direct disobedience to a
command. He should always be punished
when punishment is deserved, and even
more important, he must be punished at the
right time. If the punishment comes too
late, the horse gets punished (in his mind)
for doing the right thing, instead of the
wrong one.

To use a simple, and common, example, a
child is riding his pony across a grassy field.
The pony keeps putting his head down to
graze. When he does, the child pulls his
head up and *then* slaps him. The pony is
punished for lifting his head when the rider
asked him to. The child is teaching him, in
effect, to put his head down and keep it
down, or he will be slapped. Or to use another, more drastic example, also common:
a horse rears, his rider loosens the reins.

When the horse comes down, the rider slaps. The horse is rewarded for doing wrong (the reins are loosened when he rears) and punished for coming back down again.

The horse only understands what is happening now. He does not see ahead, nor does he consciously look back. He forms habits, very readily, but they are not conscious habits. He does not think them over, he does them because he has done them before. He repeats pleasant actions, and tries to avoid unpleasant ones. Thus the rider must be very careful that the things he wants the horse to do are pleasant, and the things he does not want him to do are unpleasant. To a horse a reward can be merely the cessation of a demand. When the rider, or handler, gives a command, he is putting a demand on the horse, by pressure on a part of the body (reins on the mouth, legs on the sides, or halter on the nose, etc.) by inclination of the body weight, etc. Even the voice is a demand, because it is reinforced by the body. The horse responds to the demand by making some movement. If he moves and the demand continues, he may continue to move, or move in another direction, or if nothing he does relieves the pressure, he may stop any movement at all. When relief does occur, the horse associates it with the action he was performing at the instant the release occurred, and that is the action he learns to repeat. His reward for obeying the signal is the end of that signal. If he is not rewarded, he does not want to repeat the action, and he fails to learn the signal. If a signal is given repeatedly and nothing that the horse does relieves it, he may learn to ignore that signal completely. For example, if you squeeze with your legs to ask the horse to move forward, and he does move, you release the squeeze. The release of the pressure rewards him for moving, and while his mind may not record it that way, he nevertheless learns that movement makes the squeeze go away, so he moves.

On the other hand, if you squeeze and he moves, but you continue to press, he hasn't accomplished anything by moving. He may move faster, which may make you stop. If this works, then he learns that the signal means to go fast. Then again, he may try slowing down to make you stop, and if you get tired at that point and stop squeezing, you have taught him to slow down instead of speed up. The signals must be timed to coincide with the actions of the horse in order to be effective and to teach the horse the correct things.

A horse can be taught to do practically anything, to a variety of signals, if the person doing the training times his rewards and punishments accurately. Relief from demands must come immediately upon the right action, and a good action must always result in some kind of reward. This is the secret to a horse that performs willingly and easily. A horse cannot be forced to do something, because in order to force a large animal such as a horse to perform, he must be intimidated. A horse cannot perform well when he is afraid, because he loses what sense of order and reason he has and becomes confused, relying on his instincts instead of his habits. And his instinct tells him to flee, not to perform.

If you understand how the horse thinks, and are always careful to reward him for the right things, and not for the wrong ones, you should be able to handle your horse calmly and sensibly. With time and patience your horse should become just as calm and sensible, even if he started out being hard to handle.

19

Leading

IT WOULD SEEM, at first, that handling the horse in the stable would be the least of the owner's problems, but in fact many problems with horses begin with handling in the stable area. Often people pay little attention to the way their horses behave in the stall and stable area, and then wonder why they are so difficult to manage under saddle and in hand.

Before you can expect to be able to control the horse from his back, you must be able to control him on the ground. Moreover, before you can train him to be ridden, and get him to be mannerly when ridden, he must be trained to be mannerly and easy to control on the lead rope. And this training begins the moment you bring the horse off the trailer into his new home. There is no substitute for this good basic training, and without it no horse can be expected to be safe and enjoyable under saddle.

You should decide just what kind of horse you want your mount to be, as far as manners are concerned. You need to set a goal and work to achieve that level of training with your horse. You should expect the horse to have good manners when you are handling him on the ground as well as when you are in the saddle. I know dozens of people who allow their horses to do all kinds of things in the stable that are irritating and unnecessary, simply because they never stopped to think that they could teach the horse not to be that way.

A horse does not have to be pushy and get in the way while you are working around him. You may not particularly mind having to dodge him as he goes in and out, and having him hang over your shoulder while you walk through the paddock, or even having to duck as he nuzzles up against you every time you turn around, but if you broke him of these little habits you would find it much easier to do your stable work and your horse's overall behavior would improve.

I don't know how many times I have had

young riders (and some not-so-young ones, too!) come to see me and ask for help, saying that they are having trouble with their horses running away, being generally hard to handle and troublesome to ride, and when I go out to investigate, I find the same things. The horse, long before you ever go to get on him, is pushy, aggressive and bossy. He tries to walk all over you, pushing against you, refusing to stand still, etc. He is usually hard to lead, walks around restlessly when tied, and won't stand to be mounted. When I see a horse act like this I can predict just how he will act under saddle, because if he doesn't have any manners on the ground, he won't have them under saddle, either.

The first step in teaching a horse ground manners is teaching him to lead properly. Once you have control of him on the lead, it is easy to progress to obedience off the lead in the stable. A horse should be responsive on the lead line, just as a well-trained dog is obedient on the leash. You will enjoy your horse much more if he is obedient and well mannered.

Your horse has to learn to go where you want him to when he is on the lead. This does *not* mean that he must learn to follow you. Teaching a horse to follow you does not teach him to lead. It merely teaches him that he can follow you if he wants to. Any horse learns readily that he doesn't have to go with you just because you get out in front of him and pull—you can't possibly make him move if he doesn't want to, unless he is a Shetland pony and you weigh 250 pounds.

The horse learns two lessons on the lead: to go when you tell him, and to stop when you tell him. Most horses are taught to lead

Leading at the walk. The horse is moving with me, not behind. I hold the shank near the halter with my right hand, with the loose end in my left.

at a very early age, which is desirable. But sometimes a horse is taught incorrectly at that age, and he spends several years practicing the wrong lesson, until it becomes very hard to change his habits to the right ones. Nonetheless, any horse can be taught to lead correctly, even a grown one that has never been halter-broken.

The first thing you must do with your horse is to get him to trust you. You should work with him until he will stand quietly

Leading at the trot. Though the horse's head is more extended, I am not pulling on the halter, and he is still moving with me, not behind.

Teaching the horse to stand for examination is useful even if you don't show. The voice command "stand" comes in handy for many things, such as getting the horse to stand quietly or even untied for grooming, shoeing, vetting, etc.

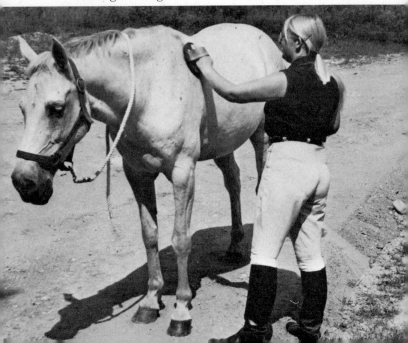

while you go all over him with your hands, not flinching away from your contact. You can start by tying him up to do this, and then get so that you can do it with him standing loose, with the lead line dangling or lying over his neck. Getting the horse to stand quietly, loose, while you work with him is the first step towards teaching him to obey you. Get him to let you pick up all four feet, groom him, etc. while he is standing loose. Use the voice command "Whoa" (pronounced "HO!") or "Stand" liberally, in a soothing tone of voice. The emphasis is on getting him to stand still. He should learn that just because you move doesn't mean he has to.

Once the horse is used to your handling him outside the stall and will stand when you handle him without being tied, you can start to work on teaching him to lead. At this point it is possible to teach him several lessons at one time, lessons which will apply throughout every phase of training and handling yet to come.

With a crop, short whip, or switch from a tree, you can now teach the horse to lead, and to move away from the whip, which will translate into moving away from your leg when the horse is ridden. You also teach him to respond a light pull on the halter, forward to go with you, and backward to stop. You want the horse to move with you, not after you. Later you will teach him to move out away from you, when you work on longeing. You will teach the horse that the voice command "Walk" and a tug on the halter mean to move.

Since it is obvious that we can't pull the horse forward if he doesn't want to go, how do we get him to move forward? Stand beside the horse's shoulder on the left side, holding the lead rope in your right hand and the whip in your left, with the business end of it pointing towards the horse's hindquarters. It might be wise to have the horse in some sort of pen, and to position him with a fence on the other side so he is not tempted to swing his hindquarters away from you. Standing thus, give a short, definite tug on the lead shank in a forward direction. At *exactly* the same time, tap the horse on the flank or quarters with the whip, give the voice command "Walk" in a commanding voice, and begin walking. If the signals you give are definite and coordinated, almost any horse will begin walking with you right then.

One thing must happen when the horse moves forward, in order for this lesson to

have been effective. You must stop all the
signals except the walking as soon as he
steps forward. This is his reward for moving
with you.

If the horse does not start forward with
you, continue the signals with more emphasis until he does. If the horse balks (plants
his feet and refuses to move) do not get out
in front of him and pull, and do not turn
around to face him. Use the whip more
strongly until he moves away from it. When
he does move, go with him and stop the
signal with the whip.

When the horse has learned to lead correctly and willingly, from both sides, you
can teach him to move out in a circle around
you on a longe line (a line about 30 feet
long). You can first teach the horse to circle
you at the end of your lead shank and then
progress to a longer line. You can also have
someone lead the horse around in the circle
at the end of the line until the horse gets
the idea.

When you longe the horse, when he is
going to the left you hold the line in your
left hand and the longe whip (available at
the tack store) in your right. Always stay a
little towards the horse's rear when you are
asking him to move out, waving the whip at
his hindquarters, and using it if necessary,

to keep him moving. Always use voice commands loudly when you are longeing, as one of the purposes of this is to teach the horse voice commands. When you longe to the right, hold the line in your right hand the whip in the left. Step towards the horse's head when you ask for a halt, as this makes him more likely to stop. If you have trouble with the horse's pulling you around on the longe line you can either run the line under his chin for more control, or use a "snubbing post." This can be either a post or a tree with a clear area around it that you can wrap the line around if the horse takes off, snubbing him to a stop. Once you get the hang of this technique you can stop even the most rambunctious horse, without risking hurting him by using a rope over his nose.

To stop the horse when you are leading him, stop your forward motion just after you have given the voice command "Whoa!" and given a short "tap" on the halter. This should be enough to stop him, but if he doesn't stop, don't try to get in front of him, Try bracing your elbow against his neck and giving a strong jerk. If necessary, walk him into a fence or a building until he is responding to you instead of just the roadblock in front of him. (This is called using visual aids to teach the horse.) Avoid swinging him around you, as this encourages a sloppy halt and puts you in a less favorable position for control. Always try to get him to stop quickly and straight, beside you.

To trot the horse on the lead, give him a little more head than for a walk (about one to two feet of rope), and start out at a trot briskly. Do not hold tight to his head, and run out at a fast enough pace that he can get into a real trot instead of just a shuffle. Keep him at arm's length from you, and try to stay about midway between his shoulder and his head. If the horse seems to shy away from you when you begin to run, try running in place beside him at a halt and walk to get him used to it.

Practice slowing from a trot to a walk before you try to halt from a trot, until he comes down smoothly and easily. Remember that it may be necessary to use much stronger pressure on the halter to get a trotting horse to stop. If you have to use a control measure, such as putting the shank over the nose or under the chin, do so. I like to use it over the nose rather than under the chin, as I find under the chin tends to make the horse want to throw his head up. Stay near the fence to keep him straight at first, until he is stopping squarely and quickly.

20

Problems in Hand

KNOWING HOW TO lead your horse properly, and teaching him to lead the right way does not necessarily mean that he will be docile and obedient all of the time. Some horses have been allowed to get away with things for years, and it may take time to get them out of these bad habits.

The kind of horse that balks on the lead line presents a problem. No amount of pulling will get such a horse to move, unless and until he is good and ready. You may be able to wait him out and get him going when he is tired of standing still, but a better solution is to use the whip or end of the line to move him forward. Few horses will stand still very long when being switched on the backside.

The handler must remember, however, that many times a horse gets balky in the

Leading the horse without a lead shank, grasping the halter firmly on the chin strap.

Leading the horse without a halter, lead shank around the neck. Keep the shank near the horse's ears for maximum control, keep the loop around the neck snug, and hold the end of the line out of the way.

Leading without halter or shank. Keep hand close to ears and grab a big handful of mane. The hand on the nose aids control and makes stopping easier.

first place because the owner has been yanking him around all the time, and the horse decides that since he gets pulled on no matter what he does, he might as well just stand there. Therefore, the handler must make certain that when he asks the horse to move forward, and he obeys, even if too quickly, the handler must not pull

back on him. You must learn to move with
the horse at least for a few strides, to reward
him, even if he jumped forward instead of
walking. Otherwise the horse hasn't learned
his lesson.

Sometimes a horse will get into the habit
of dragging his owner all over the place.
This kind of horse seems to be insensitive
to the halter and refuses to stop or turn.
This problem often occurs when a small
child is given a large horse to control, or
even a smart little pony. The horse quickly
learns that he is bigger and stronger than
his leader.

Usually a horse that has this bad habit is
also the kind that crowds and pushes in the
stable area. He needs to be taught some
manners. He needs to be taught to respect
people, without fearing them. If the horse
has a habit of walking up to you and pushing against you when you go into the stall or
paddock, you can teach him not to do it.
Find a short stick, about 18 inches long, and
carry it with you. When the horse gets too
close, raise the stick and put it between you
and the horse at about waist level, lengthwise so the end of it pokes him. Do not
swing it or hit him with it. If you hold it
properly, he won't even associate it with

Making a control halter. Run the shank up through the halter ring, bring it over the nose and snap it to the side ring on the right side of the halter. Now the chain pulls on the horse's nose as well as the halter.

Another way: Run the shank through the side ring on the left side, bring it under the chin and snap it to the side ring on the other side. Now the shank pulls on the jaw bones, as well as on the halter noseband.

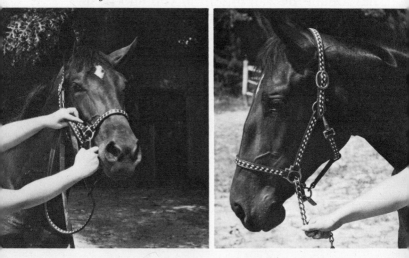

you, he'll just learn that for some reason if he gets too close something pokes him in the side, or shoulder, and hurts. He'll soon learn to be friendly, but to keep his distance.

Teaching your horse not to crowd in the pasture and stable may solve the problem on the lead automatically. However, he may still need some lessons in manners on the lead. You can make a control halter with your lead shank if you find a good hard yank will not control him. Run the lead through the halter and over the nose where the noseband lies (see pictures), under the halter, or run it under the chin so that it pulls against the jaw. If the horse is particularly bad, a shank with a chain may be needed. Do not let the lead drop down over the nose where it can cut off the wind, and do not run it through the mouth like a bit. If the horse is so bad that he needs something in his mouth and will not respond to anything else, then use a bridle. A bit will be less damaging to his mouth than a chain.

If necessary, snub the horse by wrapping the rope around a post or tree to stop him. This is also useful in stopping a horse on the longe line, as mentioned before. Also remember that short, sharp jerks are more effective than a steady pull. Use voice commands liberally when training a horse. Give the commands to speed up in a firm voice with a rising inflection: "wa-ALK!" Let your voice encourage him to go faster. When you want him to slow down, or to stop, use the opposite tone, a calm, lowering inflection. Use the same words over and over again for a command, and try to keep to one word, one syllable commands. Avoid signals like "Come on now," and "Slow down, boy." Voice commands may also help you synchronize your movements with the horse's, and to help you keep your timing. When you ask your horse to move, you must move with him, at least when you have him in hand.

Some horses have a habit of nibbling or nosing you, sometimes just putting their muzzle on you, sometimes actually biting. Even a horse that has never bitten anyone should not be allowed to do this, for it encourages him to bite, and it is particularly dangerous around your face. A horse that has been getting away with this kind of thing for a long time may be very persistent, but again, the solution is simple. Every time the horse puts his nose against you, either push him away roughly, saying "No!"

sharply, or give him a short, hard punch in the nose with your fist. Do not swing at him or wave your arms or hands around. Just bring your hand up under his nose where he can't see it coming and hit him. Don't hit him anywhere but on the end of the nose. If you do it right, he won't even realize that you have struck him, because he won't see what hit him. Make sure that you handle him around his head and neck to keep him from getting head shy, but do not allow him to put his nose on you.

Surely one of the most irritating bad habits a horse can get into is being hard to catch. It is one of those things that make us feel particularly inadequate, since we can hardly outrun the beast, and trapping him in a corner tests not only his courage but ours as well.

But hard-to-catch horses can usually be cured, even if they have been practicing their bad habit for years. They can be cured because they like to eat, and food will eventually win out over fear, or distrust, or just plain stubbornness.

The trick to catching a hard-to-catch horse is to feed him every time you catch him. Never try to catch him without something to eat (for him). After all, there's no reason why he shouldn't get a treat for allowing you to catch him, particularly since you will also probably ride him. The reason that horses get hard to catch in the first place is that they learn to associate it with work and they don't think they get anything for letting you catch them. And they learn very quickly that you can't catch them if they don't want you to.

You could carry an apple or a carrot in your hand to give your horse, but some horses are so shy of people in a field that they never get close enough to you to see the treat. And, since feeding out of your hand is encouraging him to bite anyway, it is a better idea to take a bucket with a handful of grain or two in it. If you have other horses in the pasture this may cause problems as you will undoubtedly catch all the horses except the one you want, but then again, it might encourage the reluctant one to come up to you. In fact, when I catch one of our horses in the field, I usually pretend I'm going to catch one of the ones I don't want, to get the one I'm after to come up looking for attention. Don't get lazy and put pebbles in the bucket to sound like grain, and then not give the horse his reward when you do catch him. Be honest and feed him every time you catch him, or he won't let you catch him every time.

If you have bought a horse and found out that he is hard to catch, or if you have one that has always been difficult, a little time and patience should get him to be glad to see you and let you catch him. Always give him food when you catch him, and don't always catch him to ride. Spend some time each day, if possible, catching him and then grooming or feeding him, anything but riding. Then when you go to catch him he won't know whether you want to ride or feed him, and the idea of a possible treat should entice him to you.

If the horse is the kind that runs at the sight of you and keeps right on running, you may have to put him in a small paddock for a while. Keep him there until he walks right up to you when you go out, or at least stands still while you approach. If you have to at first, keep walking after him, offering the bucket, until he gets tired or his curiosity overcomes him and you can catch him. Catch him often, and spend a lot of time just grooming him and feeding him, and make your rides as pleasant as possible. The important thing is to get your horse to think that you are pleasant and nice to be around.

If, after being patient and giving the horse a treat every time you catch him, the horse persists in leading you around the pasture in a merry chase every time you go to catch him, you may want to keep him in a small pasture all the time, so you can corner him and catch him more easily.

If you don't have the time to spend making the horse easy to catch, and if you can work it, you may want to keep him in his stall at night and ride him after you feed in the morning, taking him right out of the stall to ride. (Remember to wait at least an hour after feeding before you ride.) Or you could lock him in the stall all day and ride him in the evening, turning him out in the pasture at night. This won't make him any easier to catch, but it may be more convenient than spending all that time catching him.

Another way to get a horse to let you catch him may be never to let him in his stall to be fed without your catching him and leading him in. If it is dinner time and he knows that his feed is in the stall, his desire to get in should overcome his dislike of being caught. This may begin the catch-and-reward routine you wish to establish.

Some determined horses may even refuse to be caught in this way. If your horse refuses to let you catch him to put him away, leave him out and don't feed him at all that night. (Make sure you give him water, though.) He won't refuse food very long, and even if he won't let you catch him at the gate to lead him in, after a day or two he will surely let you walk up to him with a bucket. Of course, when you do catch him that first time, don't ride him! Catch him several times before you ride him, and then ride only a short while the first few times. This may ruin your schedule of riding or training for a time, but in the long run the time and aggravation saved by having an easy-to-catch horse will be worth it. You might also want to wait until the weather is bad and you can't ride much anyway to go through this routine of teaching him to be caught.

21

Hauling

BEFORE I GO into loading and shipping horses, I would like to discuss protective shipping equipment. Many people haul horses for years with no protective bandaging at all and have no real problems. Indeed, some horses object strenuously to bandages, tail wraps, etc. And if you do not show and seldom haul your horse anywhere, there is not too much point in investing in shipping boots, etc., unless the horse is known to be the kind that fights loading and that does not ride well.

There is one piece of equipment that I would recommend always using when hauling a horse, however. It is called a head bumper or head guard, and it is a piece of felt covered with leather on one side that fits over the horse's ears and protects the top of his head should he rear or strike it on

the top of the trailer. The halter crownpiece
fits through the keepers on the head
bumper to hold it on. At a cost of about
$5.75, it can save your horse and you a lot of
headaches.

If you are planning to haul your horse
often enough for you to feel that you need
to protect him—which, as far as I am concerned, means if you plan to haul him
more than the one time when you bought
him and the one time when you sell him—
you should learn which parts of his body
need to be protected, and how to do it.
Probably the most vulnerable part of the
horse during shipping is his legs, particularly the coronet and fetlock area. As the
horse moves around in the trailer or van to
keep his footing, he often steps over and
nicks his coronary band or hits his fetlock
joints. These scrapes and bruises can cause
lameness, and injuries in this area are often
difficult to treat and take a long time to heal.

Leg protection can vary from a simple
elastic bandage used over sheet cotton or
toweling, with or without bell boots, to
more elaborate (and more handy) shipping
boots that snap or buckle on (cost about
$9.00 to $20.00). The least expensive bandages are also the most difficult to put on,

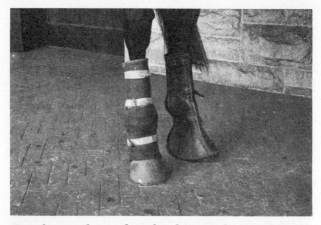

Two forms of store-bought shipping boots. They are easy to put on, but relatively expensive, and no better than bandages.

and it may take quite a while to put them on a jumpy horse. A plain Ace bandage can be used, or you can buy "track bandages" in sets in various colors. (About $4.50 a set.) The horse's legs should be wrapped from the knees and hocks down, all the way over the coronary band.

If you don't use shipping boots, you can use regular hand towels or cotton batting to cushion the bandages. Diaper pins are handy for securing the ends of the bandages. First wrap the toweling or cotton around the leg snugly. Wrap the bandage on, starting at the middle of the cannon bone and working first up to the knee, then down over the coronary band and up to the middle again. Wind the bandage tightly enough to hold the toweling in place, but not so tightly that the circulation is cut off. Work bandages used for support rather than

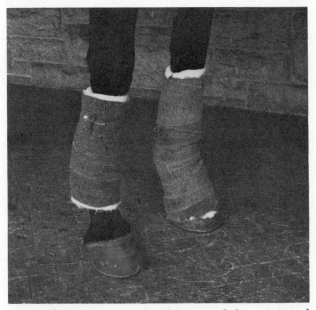

A *standing* (or *rest*) *bandage, at left, compared with a shipping bandage that covers the coronet, providing better protection.*

protection are used without any cotton or only a very thin sheet, and are wrapped a little more tightly. Running work bandages is something of an art, and you should not attempt to do it without getting some first-hand instruction from someone who is proficient at it. If the bandage is too loose, it will come down during work, but if it is too tight, or if there are any folds or wrinkles in it, you can very easily "cord" or "bandage bow" a horse. Even tail bandages can be put on too tight, and you will sometimes see white hairs at the root of a horse's tail that indicate that someone once put a tail bandage on him so tightly that he lost circulation.

The strings attached to many "track bandages" are often the site of a pressure point, and many horsemen prefer to remove them, using a pair of crossed baby safety pins to secure them instead. These are sometimes covered with masking tape in turn, to insure that they do not open accidentally.

If your horse has a habit of rubbing his hocks or kicking the tailgate of the trailer, you can wrap the bandages on the hind legs from above the hocks down. However, the horse may fret and kick even more from this, and if the bandage is too tight the

horse may walk stiffly for a time after un-
bandaging. There also are boots made especially for protecting the hocks, although
they are fairly expensive.

If you are tempted to dispense with wrapping the hind legs because the horse
doesn't stand still particularly well, remember that with step-up trailers especially, the horse will often hit the front of
the cannon bones on his hind legs when
stepping off, and this injury alone often
makes a horse refuse to load.

If your horse has a habit of rubbing his
tail on the tailgate, or if he is braided and
you want to make sure that he doesn't rub
the braiding out, you may want to wrap his
tail. Using an elastic bandage, start as close
to the top of the tail as you can and wrap
down about half the length of the tail, or
over the end of the braiding. Wrap snugly,
and pin the ends on the outside. Commercial tail guards may also be used. It should
be pointed out that padding and the proper
use of butt chains should eliminate the
problem of tail and hock rubbing in the
trailer.

You will probably get all kinds of advice
on whether or not to use sheets or blankets
during hauling. If the weather is cold and

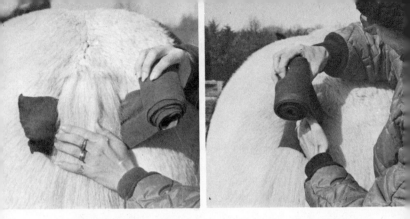

Wrapping the tail for shipping. Start the bandage as high as you can pull it under the tail. Smooth the hair first. Fold the short end over and hold it while you start to wrap, trying to keep the bandage tight so that it will not slide down the tail.

Wrap the bandage snugly, but not tight enough to restrict circulation. If the bandage is too tight, or left on too long, it may be worse than no protection at all. Wrap down to just above the end of the tail bone, and work back up, ending in a knot that can't rub out.

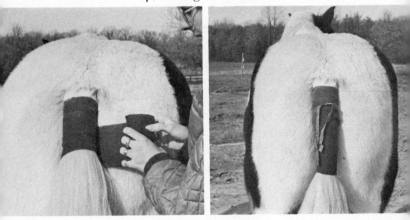

the horse is accustomed to wearing a blanket at night, for instance, then I would use a blanket to haul him. But if he had a heavy coat and I didn't have a blanket handy, I wouldn't worry about it. When I haul I generally use a lightweight sheet. It protects the horse's coat from getting rubbed and dirty if he leans on the side of the trailer, and it keeps him cleaner (for shows). If he has been sweating, or if he is a nervous sweater in the trailer, it cuts down on the possibility of chills. In the summer, unless I am going to a show, I often dispense with a sheet unless I think the trailer or van is particularly drafty. In general, unless the weather is bad, or the horse has a very light coat and it is cold, or if the horse is wet for some reason, I wouldn't worry about not having a sheet or blanket to use.

A few more words on equipment: never haul a horse with his tack on (saddle and bridle). Always carry a pocket knife somewhere easily accessible when hauling, in case an accident occurs and you have to cut the horse loose, or in case he throws a fit and hangs himself up on the feed bin.

Most horses, I am sure (or at least I hope) will go into a trailer or van with little or no coaxing. Of course the ones who won't are so irritating that we forget how many times they did it willingly. It is terribly frustrating to be all ready for a show and have the horse refuse to load, and sometimes the darn thing even refuses to go on when you are at the show and it is time to go home. Then it's not only irritating, it's embarrassing, too.

Sometimes if a horse has been hurt in a trailer or when being loaded or unloaded, it takes a long time and a lot of patience to win his confidence back. A trailer is a strange place that a horse instinctively is reluctant to enter. He knows that it is a small box which he cannot get out of easily. One of the reasons that a horse smells a trailer so carefully before entering it is probably that he wants to make sure there is nothing in it that may attack him (a snake, for instance). Anything that frightens a horse or hurts him in any way when he is in or near a trailer or van may turn him against it, and any bad experience around a trailer may make him shy of it, even if it is not related to the trailer.

Aside from fussy loading, the commonest shipping problem is the "climber"—the horse who becomes disoriented when he feels centrifugal movement, and thinks that

A two-horse, step-up trailer. Note the padding in front and on the sides, the non-skid floor mat, and the butt chains hanging at the back. The escape door on the right is big enough to let you out, but too small to encourage the horse to think about it.

he has to climb the wall to keep a floor under his feet. Once a horse has been knocked down in a van or trailer, he will very often become a climber, and it is almost impossible to overcome this fear, though tranquilizers work in a few cases. Fortunately, it is usually possible to completely avoid it by simply shipping the

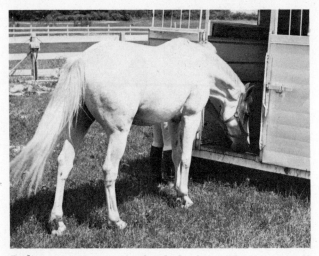

Before you attempt to load the horse, let him smell the trailer, even if he knows it.

climber in a double stall—a trailer with the partition removed, or a van with the partition or bar removed. This makes it impossible for the horse to climb, for he cannot lean far enough to lean against one side of the stall while "climbing" on the other.

The horse should be taught to go into the trailer on command, not just if he feels like it. It is the same principle as for leading: the horse should think that he must obey the command, and that something good will happen if he does. If the horse has been taught to lead correctly, to stand on command, and to tie, he will be more likely to load easily.

Whether the horse has been in a trailer before or not, he should always be given time to look it over before he is supposed to load. Even if it is his own trailer and he has been in it many times before, let him smell it. It may have changed in ways you are not aware of since the last time he was in it, and he feels he must check it before he can go in. This is an instinct so strong that you should not even attempt to overcome it. Always try to plan your activities so that you can load the horse at a leisurely pace.

Try to park the van or trailer in a familiar place while you are teaching a young horse to load, or one that has been frightened of loading. Later when the horse has gained confidence you can move to more distracting surroundings, so that when you go to shows or trail rides he will not spook at the unfamiliar area.

It may be a good idea to park the vehicle in or next to the pasture so that the horse can become familiar with it and learn to accept it as part of his domain. You can even leave it open with a little feed in it, if you block it up well enough that it will not move if the horse walks in. This way the horse may learn to go in all by himself. Do not do this if there is more than one horse in the pen, however, as they may get in and try to fight.

The horse does not have to be thoroughly used to the trailer before you try to load him, but at the same time, it may not be wise to try to load one that still shows active fear and distrust of the trailer (unless you have to, of course). A horse that shies away from a trailer may learn to trust one if the owner feeds him next to it for a few days, then when he is tied to it (if he ties dependably, otherwise he may associate fighting the rope with the trailer), and finally on the tailgate or on the back of a step-up.

Some horses may feel more confident about going in a trailer if there is already a horse in it, but make sure that you eventually teach him to go on by himself without a companion.

Always make sure the trailer is securely hitched and that the ramp is on level ground so that one side of it isn't up in the air. Check the ramp and doors to make sure they are in good condition, as well as the tires, brakes and lights. If you have a van, make sure the ramp is strong, skid-resistant,

Ideally, he should load easily, going on without you. Unfortunately, some horses never get as dependable as this one, who never gives trouble, even in a strange trailer.

and has sides. Never haul a horse in a rig you feel to be unsafe or undesirable, no matter how much you want the horse to go to that show — it isn't worth it!

A horse that has never been in a trailer before may be easier to load than one that has had a bad experience with loading. The green horse, once he has been shown that the trailer will not move, and doesn't have

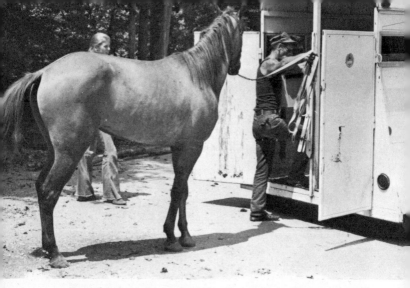

For the less-than-ideal loader, psychology is called for as well as muscle. First Jerry tries going in the other side of the trailer. (Note the longe line being used as a shank.)

Since that didn't work, I put some grain in the feed box and have the rope running out the escape door. I also have grain in my hand to entice the mare on, since she doesn't respond well to forcing.

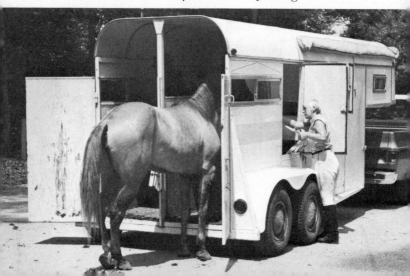

anything horrible in it, can often be led right in, particularly if he knows there is grain in the feed box. Opening the escape doors may help make him feel more comfortable, giving him the idea that it isn't closed in. Parking the trailer in a sunny spot so there is more light may also help.

From the beginning, you should expect your horse to go into the trailer without you. Walking into a trailer in front of a horse has several disadvantages. If you have taught him to lead correctly, he will naturally want to stop if you step out in front of him, especially if you turn around to face him. If you have trained your horse to stand at halter, this is an automatic signal to stand, in fact. And since a horse has an instinctive dislike of stepping on people, he may not realize you will back up, and be hesitant to walk toward you, since you block the doorway. If the horse should spook and jump forward, for instance if someone behind him slaps him on the rump when he stops, he may step on you. And if he should back up suddenly, you have much less control in front than you would at his side. Sending your horse into the trailer without you will also save problems if you have to load in a trailer with no escape door, or when there is only one door on the trailer and you are loading on the other side. In a van, you should lead the horse up the ramp and then send him into his stall.

Some horses are afraid of ramps, possibly because they're smart enough to know there's nothing under them. Try putting the horse's feed just far enough into the trailer that he has to put one or both front feet on the ramp to reach it. Once he does that, move it back until he is all the way on the ramp, and then in the trailer. Or you can try walking him across the ramp, not asking him to go into the trailer. Take your time, let him experiment. Never, never, get mad and hit him or do anything to scare him further. Once in a while you may come across a horse that refuses to load just because he is stubborn, but I think most cases of refusal are based on fear, and should be treated with patience.

If the horse refuses to load, and just stands there without moving, you may be able to use a back rope to push him on. Tie one end of a long rope (a 30-foot longe line is good) to one side of the trailer, and run it around the horse's hindquarters just below the curve of the haunches. Then you may be able to push the horse enough to get him on the trailer.

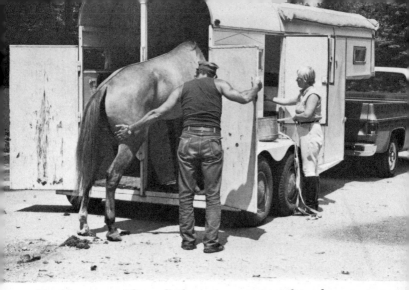

Now Jerry provides a little encouragement from behind, being careful that she doesn't suddenly back out. This was the first time this three-year-old mare loaded this easily—total time, five minutes.

Loading in the ramp trailer, we give the horse a little time to look the situation over.

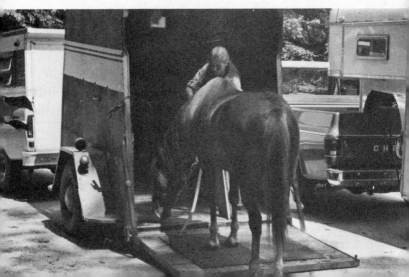

To teach the horse to go on the trailer ahead of you, stand at his shoulder with him facing the trailer as close to the back of it as you can get him. Then, lay the lead shank over his neck back by his withers, hold the halter under his chin loosely. Using your whip or stick, tap him on the side or hind-quarters, tug on the halter in a forward direction, and give your voice command to walk. Make sure there is a handful of grain in the feed box in the trailer and that the horse knows it is there. If he has a tendency

When he stubbornly refuses to go in we get after him a little. (If you were using a back rope, you'd hold it about at the level of our hands.)

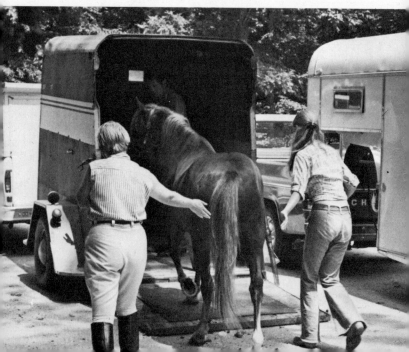

to step away from you, have someone stand on the other side of him. If you have to use a back rope to get him on, put a long lead line on him and run it through the trailer and out the door so you can pull on it as well as the back rope while you are standing next to him. This also gives you more leverage to pull in case he tries to back up.

What happens when you find yourself in the situation where you have to load the horse in a hurry, no matter what? It's usually at a show, it's getting dark, and the horse just won't go in. What then?

One solution to this problem may be to convince the horse that he is more afraid of you than he is of the trailer. This policy should be used with caution because some horses may become even worse when handled this way, although it seems to work with most horses. If the horse is the quiet, docile type that just stands there and refuses to go in, you may be able to "spank" him into the trailer. Usually the best way to do this is to first run a long rope from the halter through the trailer and out the front door back to you or someone helping you. The long line gives you more leverage should the horse pull back violently.

If another long rope is available and the horse tries to sidestep away from side to side, running a back rope may help. To do this, tie one end of the rope to the back side of the trailer (or get someone big and strong to hold it) and run it around the horse's hindquarters just below the point of the buttocks, then snub it (wrap it around once) on the other side of the trailer if possible. This gives leverage so the horse doesn't pull the rope out of your hands. Then either you or

Practicing may help the horse who is afraid to step up or down with a step-up trailer. This low bank is about the same height as the trailer. I lead the horse up so that he knows how high it is.

another person can hold this rope, and help push the horse into the trailer. Both head and back ropes must be kept tight.

If pulling on the back rope doesn't get the horse in the trailer, you need to "persuade" him a little. I've found the best thing to use in such a case is usually a riding crop or the end of a leather lead shank. This will sting the horse but won't hurt him even if you get mad and really hit him with it. (Don't use

Then I back him down again. When he gets to the edge you may have to push, but keep at him until he steps down, keeping him straight. Then praise him. Horses don't like this much, but it helps give them confidence.

the chain end of a shank, though!) With some horses one good crack across the rump may be enough to convince him; with others it might take a real "spanking." Start with one hard swat, and give the horse a chance to move. If he takes even one step forward, or puts one foot in, stop and praise him for a minute. If he does not move, or if he tries to back up, hit him again. You may just have to keep spanking him until he gives up and goes in. *Remember to reward him extravagantly when he does go in.*

If this treatment seems to make the horse worse (if he starts to rear, or otherwise becomes violent), it is probably going to make things worse and you may just have to be patient and coax him in. The excitable type of horse that reacts to being forced in by panicking makes the problem more difficult, but the owner should keep in mind that he really is smarter than the horse, and sooner or later he should be able to outsmart the horse and get him into the trailer. Care should be taken when deciding what to do with this type of horse, as too much pressure could possibly just further entrench a fear and dislike of trailers in his mind. Slow, careful manipulation of a back rope accompanied by coaxing with feed may talk the horse in. Blindfolding may work with a ramp trailer, although sometimes it just confuses the horse more. If the horse is small and there are several large men around, you may be able to lift his hindquarters off the ground and carry him in. (Only works with non-kickers, needless to say!)

Then again, sometimes you come across a horse that seems to get worse no matter what you do to him. Coaxing gets nowhere, the horse rears, strikes out, kicks, and generally turns into a tornado every time you try to move him towards the trailer, much less inside it. If you are at home this is the horse that gets left for another day, but if you somehow got him to a show, you'll somehow have to get him back in the trailer.

Here is my way of handling such a horse. It has never failed me, although I am somewhat careful as to what kind of horse I use it on. First, lead the horse away from the trailer a short way and calm him down as much as possible. Then take one of your long ropes (you may have to borrow some—they are essential) and tie it in a *non-slip* knot around the horse's neck. Run the rope through the halter as you do for tying a rope-breaker. Then take another rope and tie it on the trailer and lay it out for a back rope. If possible, collar several men to help you if needed. I hope you have the horse bandaged and a head bumper on him, because he's going to need them. Next, find something to use to spank the horse, something that will hurt, even if it's a two-by-four, but not actually injure the horse (no iron pipes or chains). A stable broom is excellent.

Now walk the horse up as close to the trailer as you can get him, even if it's sideways. You want to get his head inside the back of the trailer, or as close to it as possible. Be calm and gentle, and try not to get him started fighting again, yet. Slowly run the head rope in through the trailer and out the front door, working carefully to keep him calm. Pull the head rope up and pull the horse's head as far into the trailer as you can and then tie the rope to the trailer, preferably in a knot that won't tighten when it is pulled on. It is a good idea to have a knife handy in case the horse falls and you can't untie the knot quickly.

The horse may begin to fight at this point, and if he does, wait until he has fought himself out before trying to proceed. Don't release the horse unless he falls and CAN'T

get up, or is choking, or has a leg caught in
something. When the horse is standing still
again, hopefully you can run the back rope
through the halter ring, around his hindquarters, and through the other halter ring,
although it isn't likely. If he won't stand
still, just bring the rope around his hindquarters and snug it up. Have the biggest
man there hold it as tight as he can. (If the
horse turns sideways you'll have to release
the rope and straighten him up again.)

Take your time and get the horse lined
up. If he fights the back rope, hold it steady
until he stops. As his head is tied, he
shouldn't be able to rear or back up,
although he may try. The rope around his
neck will keep him from breaking the halter
and will help keep his head down.

By this time a lot of horses give up and
get on the trailer, but if yours is one that
won't, you will have to start to get rough. If
the owner of this horse is a child or someone who might get upset at seeing his horse
royally clobbered, it might be a good idea to
have him/her leave the scene until the
horse is in the trailer. Indeed, often the
problem exists because the owner has allowed the horse to "buffalo" him into letting him get away with things like balking

at the trailer. At any rate, the time has come for you to teach the horse that it is a lot more pleasant inside that trailer than it is behind it.

Have everyone helping you get ready to pull on their respective ropes and close the back of the trailer the instant the horse is in. Clear everyone else out of the way. Then stand slightly to the side of the horse's hind-quarters (if he kicks he will kick back) as far away from him as you can get and still use your "persuader." Then tell your back-rope man to pull on the count of "three" and haul off and hit that horse on that count. Hit him on the fleshy part of the haunches *as hard as you can.* Even if you are a big man, you will not injure the horse, unless you are using something really heavy, which I hope you aren't. If one swat doesn't do it, then you will just have to keep at it until he goes in. If the horse is snubbed down tightly and the back rope is applied strongly, he just can't go anywhere but in the trailer. And if you've hit him hard enough, he *will* go in.

Once the horse is in the trailer, lock the back, throw the ropes in or give them back, and pull off as soon as you can, to get the horse's mind off his sore behind.

A few words of caution in this business.

This may not be the best way of handling an expensive show horse, as he may hurt himself. You'll have to decide whether or not it's worth the risk. I do not recommend doing this to a young horse (under three years old). It is a last resort only, and may do permanent harm to a youngster's feelings about trailers. And I would not attempt to try it unless I had the time, people and ropes available to do it right.

The next time you try to load a horse that has had this treatment, it might be a good idea to assume you'll have to do it all again, just in case. Some horses just never seem to learn. However, I might add that almost every horse I have ever done this to or seen it done to will load almost instantly ever after, just at the sight of ropes and a crop (or whatever). On the rare occasions when it makes a horse worse, it might be wise to consider either selling the horse or giving up going to shows.

With the excitable horse that rears and jumps around, the problem is often more complicated. Tranquilizers, if available, may be helpful. Hitting or trying to rush the horse usually makes him worse, and he may injure himself and you if he really panics. Slow, careful manipulation of a back rope accompanied by much reassuring talking and petting may work. Blindfolding him may work, and just plain outlasting his patience may do it. Getting mad and clobbering him usually is the worst thing you can do with a horse like this. Generally, it is best to look the situation over and use your ingenuity. Remember, you really are smarter than the horse is.

Another thing that sometimes happens with loading is the horse that goes in fine, but comes right back out, fast. When you are at a place where time is short, I suggest padding him up well and getting a few husky fellows to close the tailgate on him before he can get his hind feet out. If he is the kind that runs out before you get the tailgate all the way down, taking the butt chains with him in some cases, put a long lead line on him before you open the door, untie him, and when you open the door or let down the tailgate, let him go out. You will still have hold of the end of the rope, so he can't get away.

If you have this kind of horse, you may want to take a few days at home and load him several times, letting him come back out on his own. He will soon get tired of it and stay in, particularly if you put his morn-

ing feed in the trailer. When he will stay in
the trailer on his own, calmly lock him in. If
he fights, it is usually best to leave him in,
let him fight it out, and when he stops, then
let him out. This way he learns that fighting
won't automatically get you to let him out.
If you are afraid that he will hurt himself, or
if he gets tangled up in something, then you
will have to let him out. Usually if you just
ignore him when he fights he will quit
doing it, as it doesn't accomplish anything.

As far as tying the horse in the trailer is
concerned, often it is more convenient to
leave him untied. However, it depends on
whether the trailer is built so that he cannot
get his head turned around. If this is the
case and there are no other horses in the
trailer, there is really no reason to tie him,
and it saves time not having to untie him
when you are ready to unload and he is impatient. Of course, if you put a short chain
with a snap on both ends in your trailer and
snap one end to the halter and one to the
trailer, the horse is tied and there are no
knots to worry about. Some horses feel more
secure if they are tied, and it gives them
something to brace on.

If your trailer has butt chains (and it
should), use them. They keep the horse

from leaning on the tailgate, support the centerboard, and give you a chance to lower the ramp or open the doors before the horse starts out.

Do not bed the trailer with hay or straw, as it will be slippery. Put a non-skid floor mat on the floor and on the ramp.

When you unload, untie the horse before you open the doors, and let him come off at his own speed. Sometimes a horse will resist coming off the trailer. If the horse has had difficulty backing off a ramp or if he has hit his legs stepping off a walk-up trailer, he may be afraid to back off.

I have found that the quickest and most effective way to handle this situation in most cases is to put long lines on the horse and drive the horse off. This can be done by attaching a line (12 feet) or longer on each side of the halter, or by running a long line (about 30 feet) through the halter ring. If you use one line, tie a knot on either side of the halter ring to keep it from slipping through. Running one rein on each side of the horse, stand a safe distance behind the trailer and walk him back. If you pull his head down to his chest and pull hard enough, you will pull him off balance and he will step back to keep from falling down.

This method has several advantages over the other alternatives, which are getting in the trailer and trying to push the horse out, or opening the doors and trying to scare him out. First of all, using the driving reins gets you out of the trailer where you are in no danger if the horse throws a fit. And it puts you in a position of control no matter how fast he comes out, or even if he falls out.

It is a good idea to ride in your trailer or van at least once, to check for loud rattles and draughts. Sometimes tin partitions rattle like cannon fire when the trailer is moving, and it may be worthwhile to replace them with wire mesh to save your horse a lot of headaches. Homemade trailers are often very noisy. It is difficult to expect a horse to perform well at a horse show if he has been riding in the middle of the Civil War on the way to the show.

Before you ship a horse in your own trailer, practice driving it without any horses in it, until you get used to making curves and corners, and backing it up. Backing a trailer is really not that hard, once you figure out what I call the formula for it. The way I do it seems a little silly, but it is the only way I can do it right. Before I start backwards, I first straighten out the wheels on the car. Then I figure out which way I want the back of the trailer to go, then which way the front of it must go, and the way the back of the car has to go to do that. Simple? Yes, but it takes practice. If you try it with a horse in the trailer and you goof it up, the horse is going to be sea sick before you get through.

When you haul a trailer with a horse or horses in it, or a van, remember that they are standing back there with nothing to hold on to. Make all your starts and stops gradual. Try not to brake in the middle of a turn, as a horse has trouble bracing sideways and front-to-back at the same time.

If your trailer is not drafty, you can put hay in it for your horse to munch on. If it blows around, however, he is better off without it, as it may get in his eyes or cause respiratory problems.

Take out any unused hay or grain after each trip in the trailer. Otherwise mice may make a home in it. If you haven't used your trailer in a while, always check the inside very carefully for hornets' nests, as they will sometimes move in within a matter of weeks.

Part IV

THE MARE AND FOAL

22

Breeding the Mare

IF YOU OWN a mare, you may at some time decide to breed her. When you do, you will want to take several things into consideration. Very young mares (two to three years) may be difficult to settle (get in foal) and may have difficulty carrying the foal and delivering due to immature reproductive organs. Remember that a horse does not mature until about age five. A well-built, well-developed three or four year old may be bred with good results, although it may be safer to delay the event a year or two.

Aged mares (over ten years) should be examined by a vet if you are considering trying to breed. A mare of this age that has produced in the last few years may be bred with good results, and may continue to produce into her twenties. However, a mare over ten years old that is maiden (has never had a foal) may be difficult, if not impossible, to settle. The condition of the mare in relation to her age will no doubt be the deciding factor. A sickly, unthrifty mare should not be bred at any age, while a robust, well-built, healthy mare can often be used into her 'teens.

A mare's conformation should be taken into account if you are considering breeding her. The foal's conformation will be inherited from both the dam and the sire, and a poorly built mare will not produce an outstanding foal no matter how good the stallion is, with rare exceptions. Mares with weedy conformation, particularly those that are very narrow and light boned in the hindquarters, may have difficulty foaling. Sometimes a mare that has a lameness that makes her unfit for riding can be bred. However, a vet should always be consulted in a case like this to determine whether foaling would cause suffering or injury to her. For instance, a stifle or hip injury could make it difficult for her to stand being bred and the mechanics of foaling.

If the mare has a serious conformation fault which could be hereditary, it may influence you against continuing the defect into another generation.

If the mare is a cribber or windsucker,

remember that the foal may learn this vice from his mother.

If the mare is blind in one or both eyes, have the vet examine her to try to determine whether the blindness was caused by injury or disease. Some causes of blindness may be hereditary.

The next step in the process of deciding to breed the mare is choosing a stallion. Your choice will probably be more heavily influenced by what is available in your area and by how much money you can afford to pay for a stud fee than by your idea of a good stallion. It is a good idea always to try to breed the mare to a stallion that is better than she is, to improve the quality of the offspring. If you have a registered mare, it would seem a waste of time to breed to a grade stallion. Crossing a registered mare out to a horse of another breed may serve the purpose of combining desirable traits of two breeds. For instance, an Arabian-Thoroughbred cross (called Anglo-Arab) is popular, and people are also experimenting with Thoroughbred-draft horse crosses for heavyweight hunters. You may want to try to find a stallion that has the qualities that you feel your mare lacks, so the foal will hopefully have her good points plus the stallion's.

If you have a grade mare, you may want to breed her to a registered horse, if you can afford the stud fee, and if there are any in your area. Some of these crosses can be registered in special registries, such as Half-Arabs, Half-Thoroughbreds, etc. You may also want to use a neighborhood stallion because of convenience.

When you choose a stallion, you want to consider his conformation as well as his bloodlines. You should be able to shop around (via breed magazines, advertisements, etc.) and find a horse with good enough conformation to make an improvement over your mare's if hers is not particularly good. Unfortunately, many mediocre horses remain stallions, and people breed their mares to them because they don't know what a good horse should look like. Before you go to find a stallion for your mare, you should try to learn enough about horses to be able to judge whether the stallion is an outstanding example of his breed. Choosing one with a good show record will help, as this is the best advertising a good stallion has.

You should also consider the temperaments of the horses involved in a breeding. For example, if your mare is rather bad-tempered you might not want to breed her to a

stallion with the same problem, but look for
one with an especially good disposition, so
the foal might be better tempered than its
mother. By the same token, if you have a
flighty horse and you would prefer the foal
to be more docile, you might want to find a
very quiet, docile stallion.

Size is another thing you should think
about. If you have a small mare and you
wish to get a larger foal, you will certainly
want to breed her to a larger horse, but
make sure there is not too great a difference
in size. A pony mare may have difficulty in
delivering a foal by a large horse.

The usual procedure in breeding a mare
is to send her to the stallion for a week or
two. When you are figuring finances, remember to include boarding and feed expenses as well as the stud fee, if any.
Always look over the facilities and type of
care given at a stud where you may send
your mare for breeding. When you arrange
for stud service, make conditions for return
of the stud fee, less expenses, if the mare
does not settle.

When you decide to breed your mare, you
will have to learn to tell when she is in
heat. This is the period when she can conceive. You are probably better off having a

vet or a breeder who has had some experience with horses help describe the signs of
heat for you, and a friend may have a mare
that you can observe during her heat period.
Once you can recognize when the mare is
in heat, you should keep an eye on her for
several months and try to determine her
schedule of heats. There is no point in
sending a mare to the stud after her heat
period is over. The mare will come in heat
once every four to six weeks, and the noticeable signs may last two weeks. If your
mare is regular and you can predict her
heats, you may want to send her to the stud
two weeks before she is due (if you can afford it) so she can get used to her new surroundings. This will help her to settle. If
she is not regular, you may just have to
watch her every day and send her on the
first or second day of her heat. Most mares
conceive on about the sixth day of heat.

You will want to pay attention to the time
of year you breed the mare. Owners with
registered horses will want to try to get a
foal as soon after January 1 as possible, as
the age of registered horses is determined
on that date. (A horse born on December 31
is officially one year old on January 1, even
though he is really only 1 day old.) As a

mare's gestation period is about 11 months, you would want to breed ideally in February or March. However, most mares have much more regular heat periods in the summer, and may not conceive in the winter. An April breeding, or early May, is usually the earliest you can depend on.

Unless you are worried about that January 1 date, you would be better off planning a May or June breeding. It puts the foal at a disadvantage to be born either in winter or in the heat of midsummer, and a May breeding will bring a spring foal. This way the foal has all summer to grow before he has to go through the cold winter months. It is easier on the mare also, as she has the new grass to feed on during the first months after foaling.

You can breed the mare one of three ways. Many large breeding farms breed artifically, the stallion ejaculating into a "boot" and the sperm injected directly into the uterus of the mare under more or less sterile conditions. This protects the mare's internal organs, may cut down on infection, and protects the stallion from possible injury. This method of breeding should be left to the experts, although your veterinarian may assist you if you desire to do it this way. The Jockey Club does not permit artificial insemination of Thoroughbreds, however.

Another method is to breed the mare in hand, that is, with someone holding the mare while another person leads the stallion up to her and allows him to mount. This helps to prevent injuries to the horses, although it may be risky to the people involved if the horses are not well trained. The mare is usually hobbled during this process to keep her from kicking, and the stallion may be muzzled if he is a biter. Most professionals use this method of breeding, and it is probably safer for the horses than field breeding. Of the man-aided methods of breeding, it is the most natural.

The easiest way to breed horses is to turn the mare and stallion into a small field and let nature take its course. This method may be the most likely to succeed in settling the mare, as neither animal is distracted by having people standing around. However, there may be danger to the stallion if the mare is a kicker. The horses should be watched the whole time they are together, and separated if necessary. If they must be separated, it is usually easier to catch the mare and lead her into another area, rather than attempting to handle the stallion when he is aroused.

It is also wise to wash the genitals of both horses involved with a mild disinfectant before breeding, and to wrap the tail of the mare. You should have the vet examine both the mare and the stallion prior to breeding. Have the mare examined internally several months before breeding. This way any infection she may have can be cleared up in time for the event.

23

Care of the Mare and Foal

ONCE YOU HAVE bred your mare, or have
bought a mare that is already in foal, there
are some things that you should keep in
mind. The foal will only be as healthy as
the mare. Keep your mare healthy, without
letting her get overly fat. Too much weight
will make it more difficult for her to foal.
Feed your mare the best quality hay, grain
and salt you can get, and you will probably
want to give her a vitamin/mineral supplement as well. (Check with your vet.)

You can ride your mare during her pregnancy until she becomes very big with foal,
about eight or nine months, depending
on how strong she is. (Ask your vet.) Exercise is good for her, but don't overdo it.
Jumping, for instance, is not wise at this
time.

If your mare is pastured with other
horses, remember that a misaimed kick can

cause her to lose the foal. If you have a persistent kicker in the field, you will be wise to separate them. Do not, however, confine the mare in a stall during her pregnancy on the grounds that roaming in the pasture may cause miscarriage. She needs regular, free exercise now more than ever. Of course, if the mare has a history of miscarriage, your vet may recommend restricted exercise. Generally, it is best to give the mare as natural an environment as possible.

When the foaling date approaches, give the mare a month's leeway in case she foals early. Or, if you don't know when she is due, watch her and assume she is near when her udder fills and her belly seems to "drop" a little. At this time, you will want to decide where you want the mare to have her foal. If you have a stall that is 14 feet square or larger (12 feet if it is a small pony) you may want to have her foal in the stall. This is an excellent place for her, provided the stall is large enough, as it is protected from both the weather and other horses, and you can keep an eye on her and help if necessary.

You may be able to block off a portion of your barn or shed for her, making sure it is large enough. A good size for a foaling box is 14′ by 24′.

If you do not have a big enough stall, you can put the mare in a paddock at night until she foals, unless the weather is bad. In rainy or very cold weather, even regular-sized stall is better than being outside. Many foals are lost each year by being dropped out in inclement weather.

If plans go well, and the weather is good, outside foaling is fine. It is a good idea to avoid leaving the mare to foal in a large pasture, as you would have trouble finding her in time to lend assistance if needed.

It is best to separate the mare from the other horses when her time is near. If you stable the mare, keep her stall as clean as possible. It is usually difficult to judge when the mare will foal. One way to tell when foaling is near is when a waxy substance forms on the udder. When this happens, it may be a few hours or two weeks, depending on the mare.

When foaling time does arrive, chances are that you will be sound asleep and will awake to a happy, healthy mare and foal. If you are on hand when she goes into labor, however, try to keep an eye on her without bothering her. Do not go in with her unless she needs help, until the foal is several hours old at least. Give the mare a chance to calm down, rest up, and accept the foal.

Some mares are very protective and will get very nasty if you try to come in too soon. Respect her wishes, and give her some time to get adjusted. If she is still nervous about you after a few days, catch her with feed and tie her up while you handle the foal. If the mare and foal are healthy, there is really no reason to handle the foal much for the first month or two.

When the mare has foaled and recovered from delivery, and the foal is up and moving about well, remove them from the area of birth to a cleaner place. Give the mare and foal a week or two to recover before turning them out to pasture with other horses.

Remember that a foal *must* nurse within an hour or two after birth. If he cannot get up to nurse by himself (he should be up within a half an hour) you will have to help him, whether the mare wants you to or not. You will probably want to call the vet if this occurs.

If the foal has not relieved himself within 24 hours of his first meal, consult your vet. He will probably recommend a warm water enema, which you can give yourself with a little help. Constipation can be a serious problem with a foal.

You may want to give your mare a bran

mash after foaling to relax her and insure that she does not get constipated. Consult your vet for a recipe and how long to wait after foaling to give it.

After the foal is born, you can feed your mare her normal feed, increasing her ration a little. Make sure she has plenty of clean water, as foaling may tend to dehydrate her. She will look as if she has lost a lot of weight after foaling. Put the mare's water and feed buckets low enough so the foal can reach them, and put the hay down where he can eat that too.

24

Weaning

YOU WILL WANT to wean the foal at about
five to six months of age, with leeway depending on the condition of the mare and
foal. If the foal is large and robust, and the
mare is a little poor, or fairly old, you may
want to wean at about four months, for instance. You will want to start the foal eating
his own ration of grain at about two to three
months, so he is eating regularly and is used
to grain and hay when he is ready to be
weaned. You may have to tie the mare up
when eating so she doesn't get the foal's
feed.

When you do wean the foal, do it completely and quickly. Trying to make it a
gradual process will only cause more anxi-
ety to the mare and foal and cause them to
go off their feed. When the time comes, put
the mare somewhere where she cannot see,

and if possible, cannot hear the foal. Feed her and try to keep her occupied. Reduce her feed ration about a third for a week or two to slow milk production.

The mare will probably adjust to the weaning process more quickly than the foal, and you should have no problems with her. The foal, however, may go off his feed for a week or two, being too worried to eat, so keep feed in front of him at all times to help keep him from losing too much weight. It is fine to put him with other horses to keep him company. If you put him with one horse, however, remember that he will become as attached to that horse as he did his mother, so you need to separate them at times also.

If your foal is a colt, you will probably want to have him gelded (castrated), unless he is registered and you plan to use him for breeding. There is some debate as to when to geld a colt. Usually the matter will be determined by how long you can go before the young stallion becomes a problem. If you have mares in the pasture he may begin to bother them at a year old. Then again, some colts don't even realize they're boys until they are two or even three years old. Some people believe in waiting until a colt is at least three or four years old before gelding, no matter how much trouble he is, on the grounds that gelding too young may stunt his growth. On the other hand, I know of at least one man who gelds all his colts as soon as their testicles drop, which is usually at about two months of age, and his colts look as good as anybody else's. If a colt's growth is impaired when he is gelded, it is probably because he has gotten infected during or after the process. Have the vet do it and take his advice on when and how to have it done, and be careful in your after care to help prevent infection.

Raising a foal can be a challenging and interesting affair. It is a good idea to halter break and teach the foal to lead while he is small enough to be handled easily, usually at about two to three months. It will be much easier for you, for instance, if he has been taught these things before he is weaned. Do not, however, ask too much in the way of learning from a colt until he is about a year old, as his attention span is very short and his muscles undeveloped. When he is about a year old you can start teaching him to longe and ponying him. Avoid spoiling the foal by letting him nip or kick. Discourage him from following you around like a dog, and teach him early that he cannot play games with you or hurt you.

A few sturdy, big boned foals may be big enough to ride at two years of age, but most will do better if you wait until they are two and one-half or three before you actually ride them. You can spend the six months prior to this teaching him to longe, teaching him voice commands, and getting him used to wearing a saddle and bridle.

Parts of the Horse

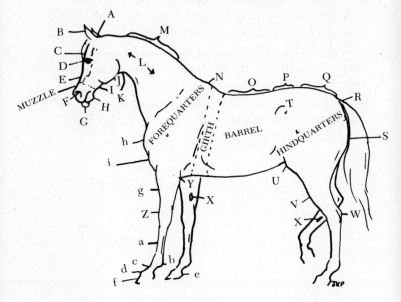

A. Poll	J. Cheek	S. Haunches
B. Ears	K. Throatlatch	T. Point of Hip
C. Forehead	L. Neck	U. Stifle
D. Eye	M. Crest	V. Gaskin
E. Face	N. Withers	W. Hock
F. Nostril	O. Back	X. Chestnut
G. Lips	P. Loins	Y. Elbow
H. Chin	Q. Croup	Z. Knee
I. Jaw	R. Dock	

a. Cannon Bone	d. Coronet	g. Forearm
b. Fetlock	e. Heel	h. Point of Shoulder
c. Pastern	f. Hoof	i. Chest

GLOSSARY OF TERMS

1. ANATOMICAL TERMS

Forequarters. Refers to the parts of the horse's body from the girth area forward, as a whole. Approximately 2/3 of the horse's weight rests on the forequarters when he is standing still; when in motion, this varies depending on what he is doing and how fast he is going.

Hindquarters. Refers to the rest of the horse, although more often it means the parts from the loin back, as a whole. The hindquarters produce the thrust to move the horse forward, sideways, and backward. Thus the horse is a "rear engined vehicle."

Poll. The area directly behind the ears.

Occipital crest. The bony top of the head between the ears.

Throttle. (Also *throatlatch.*) Where the neck meets the head. When the horse flexes at the poll, he bends his neck in this area. The extent to which he can become flexible here depends on how cleanly his head joins the neck; thus a thin, smooth throttle is desirable.

Crest. The top part of the neck forming more or less of an arched effect; where the mane grows.

Withers. The rise at the end of the neck where the shoulder blades of the horse meet and the vertebrae of the back begin. The place from which a horse is measured. Where the front of the saddle rests when placed in position for riding.

Point of the shoulder. The forward-most point of the side of the horse, on either side of the chest.

Shoulder. That area extending roughly from the point of the shoulder to the withers, and down to the elbow, for purposes of external identification.

Elbow. The uppermost joint in the leg, which is below the withers when the horse is standing squarely. When riding your toe will be close to the elbow. The joint corresponds to the human knee in construction.

Forearm. The area between the elbow and the knee of the horse, having several large muscles.

Knee. The joint approximately halfway down the horse's front leg. Corresponds to the human ankle. Should be straight, wide when viewed from the front, flat in front when viewed from the side.

Chestnut. The callous-like bump on the inside of all four legs, in the front above the knee, in the rear below the hock. Supposedly the last vestiges of prehistoric toes in horses.

Cannon bone. The bone between the knee and fetlock joint. The hard substances behind the cannon bone which are sometimes mistaken for bones are actually tendons and ligaments. There are no muscles below the knees and hocks of horses.

Fetlock (Fetlock joint.) The hair which grows on the back of the joint is called the fetlock. The joint, which is the joint below the knee, corresponds to the human digits of the foot.

Pastern. The area between the fetlock and the hoof. A continuance of the system of digits of the lower leg.

Coronet. (Coronary band.) Where the hair of the leg stops and the hoof begins, the coronet forms something of a ridge. The hoof grows from this band.

Heart. The horse's heart can be felt just inside the left elbow. The term heart also refers to courage or stamina of the horse.

Loins. The area of the spine between the back and the croup, behind the ribs and in front of the hip. The weakest part of the horse's back; the kidneys lie under the spine at this point.

Coupling. (Coupled.) Where the loins join the hindquarters. A horse is said to be short coupled when this area is compact and there is a small space between the last rib and the stifle.

Barrel. The middle of the horse, his ribcage.

Croup. The area between the loins and the tail.

Dock. The tail at its juncture to the body.

Point of the hip. The bony protuberance which is the front of the pelvis, on each side. The croup is measured from this point to the tail.

Buttocks, haunches. The curve at the back of the hindquarters which is the rearmost point of the pelvis.

Stifle. The joint below the point of the hip, approximately parallel with the elbow. Corresponds to the human knee.

Gaskin. The area between the stifle and the hock.

Hock. The joint in the hind leg which is parallel to the knee in front, which also corresponds to the ankle joint in the human.

(The joints below the hock are the same as in the forelegs.)

Sheath. In geldings and stallions the sheath holds the penis and is located between the hind legs approximately between the stifle joints.

Udder. In mares the udder is found high between the hind legs.

2. COMMON CONFORMATION TERMS

Roman nosed. When the profile of the face is convex rather than straight.

Dished face. When the profile is concave.

Lop ears. When the ears tend to hang outward rather than stay straight. Normally the ears move forward and backward rather than out to the side.

Pig eyes. When the eyes are small and deep set, rather than being large, alert and intelligent looking.

Ewe necked. When the neck seems to be concave instead of having at least a little arch to it. The middle of the neck seems to be fallen in.

Straight shoulder. When the angle of the shoulder is not acute enough; the withers seem to be directly over the elbow instead of somewhat behind the elbow. When a horse has a good shoulder, his back on top seems to be much shorter than the line between his elbows and his stifle.

Mutton withered. The horse seems to have no withers, they are very flat and wide.

Narrow chest. There is not enough room between the front legs and the points of the shoulders.

Over at the knee. The knee seems to be perpetually bent to some degree, the straight line down the front of the leg to the fetlock is broken.

Back at the knee, calf-kneed. The leg seems to be bent backward at the knee.

Straight pasterns. There is not enough angle between the pastern and the fetlock joint.

Goose rumped. Too much slope in the croup; tail set too low.

Wasp-waisted, herring gutted. When the underline of the barrel seems to run up towards the tail and the horse has a very small abdominal space.

Slab-sided. The rib cage is not sprung well enough; the horse is too flat in the sides.

Sickle-hocked. There is too much angle in the hock joint. Instead of dropping straight, the cannon bone in the hind leg slants forward when the horse is standing naturally.

Cow-hocked. When viewed from the rear the hocks seem to be closer together than the hips or the feet.

Weedy. A general term meaning that the horse does not have enough substance; the horse seems to be too lightly built to carry much weight or do much work.